A COMPLETE MATHS PROG[RAMME]
FOR PRIMARY SCHO[OLS]

Planet Maths

4th Class
Satellite Activity Book
Liam Gaynor

FOLENS

Author: Liam Gaynor
Editor: Finola McLaughlin
Design: Marian Purcell
Layout: Marian Purcell
Illustrator: Brian Fitzgerald
Photographs: Thinkstock

ISBN: 978-1-84741-787-9

© Folens Publishers, 2011

First published in 2011 by: Folens Publishers,
Hibernian Industrial Estate, Greenhills Road, Tallaght, Dublin 24.
Produced in Ireland by Folens Publishers.

The paper used in this book is sourced from managed forests.

Folens books are protected by international copyright laws. All rights reserved. The copyright of all materials in this book, except where otherwise stated, remains the property of the author(s). No part of this publication may be reproduced, stored in a retrieval system or transmitted in any form or by any means (stencilling, photocopying, etc.) for whatever purpose, even purely educational, without the prior written permission of the publisher. The publisher reserves the right to change, without notice, at any time the specification of this product. The publisher has made every effort to contact copyright holders but if any have been overlooked we will be pleased to make any necessary arrangements. To the best of the publisher's knowledge, information in this book was correct at the time of going to press. No responsibility can be accepted for any errors.

Introduction for Parents and Teachers

Planet Maths is a series of Maths textbooks, activity books and corresponding teacher's manuals for Junior Infants to 6th Class. It is in line with the Revised Primary Curriculum and has been written by primary school teachers. Curriculum Strands, Strand Units and Objectives are detailed throughout. Blue teaching boxes introduce new concepts as they arise.

Planet Maths has been designed to provide students with challenging activities and enjoyable mathematical experiences to help them become confident mathematicians. Pupils using **Planet Maths** will experience mathematical learning through the following approach:

- Learning the new maths skills associated with a topic with the aid of explanation boxes and/or worked examples that introduce each new concept or operation;
- Practising and reinforcing new skills through drills and repetition, while also providing as much variety and stimulation as possible;
- Exploring and applying their skills in 'real life' contexts and situations that are relevant, fun and stimulating to young minds.

'Real life' themed maths features

There are seven two-page 'real life' themed maths features spread throughout the 3rd to 6th Class textbooks. They are **designed to bring Maths to life**, making it more engaging for students by enabling them to use their skills in contexts that are **refreshing**, **relevant** and **interesting** to them. Each 'real life' feature uses the skills and knowledge that pupils have acquired in the preceding units.

Warm-Up Activities

A warm-up activity appears at the beginning of every new topic along with the instruction, 'Listen to your teacher'. These game-like activities open each unit of the senior textbooks and are led by the teacher with directions from the accompanying teacher's manual. Because they are conducted at the start of each unit, these activities provide a **mental warm-up** for students, preparing them to learn by focusing their attention on the teacher. Warm-up activities are based on the **concepts** and **operations** relevant to the topic.

Pair and Group Work

The series recognises the value of collaborative learning and **ample opportunities** are provided throughout the textbooks for both pair work and group work. Maths puzzles suited to pairs, straightforward group activities and oral activities such as 'pretend you are the teacher' are used in the series.

Differentiation

To promote ease of differentiation, a **red line** appears beside a selection of problems and sums in the 3rd to 6th Class textbooks that could prove more challenging for many pupils. Additionally, the 3rd to 6th Class textbooks contain **Challenge Yourself** problems designed to provide early finishers with extra stimulus and reward, and to assist with differentiation.

Self-Assessment

Self-assessment is strong feature of the series. Pupils are encouraged to rate their own performance and understanding of a topic through the use of a **traffic light system** at the end of every page in each topic. Students can assess their performance at the end – red for difficulty, amber for improvement and green for full understanding.

Check Up Activities

Each topic unit concludes with a page of concise check up activities designed to reinforce learning. Check ups include **oral, operational, problem-solving** and **shared activities** based on the topic at hand. Oral activities reinforce **communicating and expressing as a mathematical skill**, and vocabulary-based exercises assess the pupil's understanding of the mathematical language used in the unit.

Mental Maths

Seven dedicated Mental Maths units are placed strategically throughout the 3rd to 6th Class textbooks, with each one including a **Multiple Choice** component. Each section in Mental Maths contains a **score box for pupils to rate their performance**. This will encourage them to collaborate in their own progress and to recognise areas where more effort and assistance is needed.

The Teacher's Manual accompanying this textbook includes:

- A guide providing comprehensive suggestions on how to make the best use of this series.
- Oral and mental maths activity suggestions.
- Maths language relevant to each topic.
- Suggestions for using concrete materials and manipulatives.
- Photocopiable activities for differentiation and extension exercises.
- Photocopiable templates for practice and repetition of fundamental concepts.
- Answers.
- Assessment sheets.
- Individual student profile sheets.
- Class record sheets.

The activity books in the series contain supplementary and differentiation activities. Interactive activities for this series can also be found at: www.folensonline.ie.

Contents

Topic		Page
1.	Place Value	5
2.	Addition	8
3.	Time	11
4.	Lines and Angles	14
5.	Subtraction	17
6.	Fractions	20
7.	Graphs	23
8.	Multiplication	26
9.	Division	29
10.	Decimal Numbers	32
11.	Money	35
12.	Symmetry	38
13.	Length	41
14.	Long Multiplication	44
15.	Fractions 2	47
16.	Chance	50
17.	Division 2	53
18.	Decimals 2	56
19.	Weight	59
20.	2D Shapes	62
21.	Patterns	65
22.	Length and Perimeter	68
23.	Area	71
24.	Time 2	74
25.	Operations	77
26.	Capacity	80
27.	Problem Solving	83
28.	3D Shapes	86
29.	Number Sentences	89
30.	Problem Solving 2	92

TOPIC 1 Place Value

A. Warm up!

1. Round each number to the nearest hundred.

   (a) 493 _____   (b) 128 _____   (c) 863 _____   (d) 76 _____   (e) 139 _____

   (f) 662 _____   (g) 8,305 _____   (h) 4,444 _____   (i) 6,789 _____   (j) 1,650 _____

2. Round each number to the nearest thousand.

   (a) 6,100 _____   (b) 2,300 _____   (c) 8,700 _____   (d) 4,800 _____   (e) 3,890 _____

   (f) 1,120 _____   (g) 4,618 _____   (h) 3,789 _____   (i) 2,159 _____   (j) 9,087 _____

B. Calculate!

1. Draw a ring around the greatest number in each set.

   (a) 156, 651, 561   (b) 808, 880, 888   (c) 138, 831, 381

   (d) 2,574, 2,698, 2,377   (e) 7,933, 7,415, 7,888   (f) 9,615, 9,621, 9,613

2. Tick the smallest number in each set.

(a)	(b)	(c)	(d)	(e)	(f)
☐ 513	☐ 1,594	☐ 2,387	☐ 5,115	☐ 6,006	☐ 8,003
☐ 531	☐ 1,965	☐ 2,873	☐ 5,511	☐ 6,600	☐ 8,300
☐ 351	☐ 1,685	☐ 2,738	☐ 5,151	☐ 6,666	☐ 8,303
☐ 315	☐ 1,758	☐ 2,299	☐ 5,551	☐ 6,606	☐ 8,030

3. Write these sets of numbers in order. Start with the smallest number.

   (a) 459, 203, 888

   (b) 951, 159, 591

   (c) 9,800, 9,100, 9,700

   (d) 4,519, 4,563, 4,528

   (e) 2,600, 4,900, 3,600

   (f) 9,800, 3,400, 8,500

   (g) 6,750, 6,790, 6,730

   (h) 7,512, 7,508, 7,580

C. Greatest numbers

1. In each set of numbers, write the number where 6 has the greatest value.
   - (a) 160, 640, 936 _____
   - (b) 4,610, 6,113, 9,006 _____
   - (c) 6,118, 1,648, 3,268 _____
   - (d) 6,042, 8,611, 7,136 _____
   - (e) 1,126, 1,362, 1,618 _____
   - (f) 7,263, 8,632, 9,286 _____

2. In each set of numbers, write the number where 3 has the greatest value.
   - (a) 321, 123, 231 _____
   - (b) 3,214, 4,318, 5,813 _____
   - (c) 1,530, 1,350, 1,503 _____
   - (d) 5,632, 3,200, 9,993 _____
   - (e) 2,613, 2,316, 2,136 _____
   - (f) 8,381, 4,434, 9,223 _____

D. True or false?

1. 4,007 = 47 ☐ true ☐ false
2. 0803 = 803 ☐ true ☐ false
3. 5,236 > 5,326 ☐ true ☐ false
4. 8,005 < 8,050 ☐ true ☐ false
5. I can make 6 different 3-digit numbers with the numerals 5, 7 and 8. ☐ true ☐ false
6. 4,006 is ten greater than 3,096. ☐ true ☐ false
7. If I round 8,189 to the nearest hundred I get 8,000. ☐ true ☐ false
8. One unit less than two thousand is one thousand, nine hundred and ninety. ☐ true ☐ false

E. Puzzles

1. Write each number in words.
   - (a) 459 _____
   - (b) 4,060 _____
   - (c) 7,000 _____
   - (d) 3,127 _____

2. To what numbers do the arrows on the number line point?

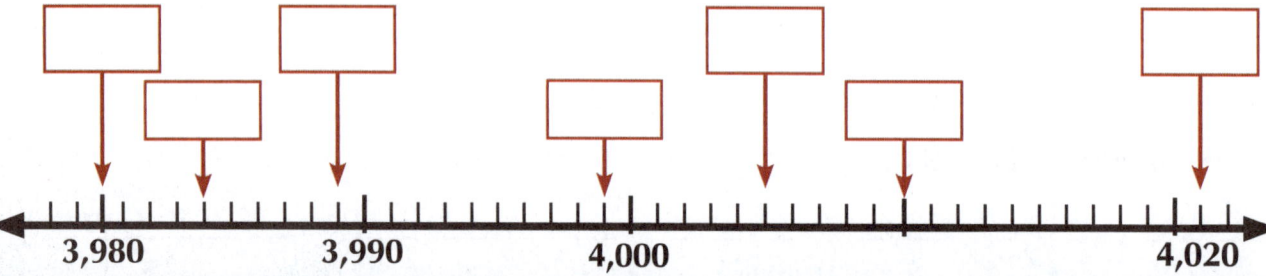

D. Addition

1. ThHTU	2. ThHTU	3. ThHTU	4. ThHTU	5. ThHTU	6. ThHTU
3124	4007	1554	3636	6422	8
1102	153	2307	1515	89	458
+ 2329	+ 2288	+ 3180	+ 2304	+ 1777	+ 9255

7. (a) 2456 + 2311 + 1155 = _____
   (b) 471 + 2116 + 3277 = _____
   (c) 7412 + 236 + 94 = _____
   (d) 1488 + 2346 + 3049 = _____

E. Calculator time

Use a calculator to check if the answers are right ✓ or wrong X.

1. 4,126 + 895 + 1,953 = 6,974 ☐
2. 3,957 + 2,666 + 2,474 = 9,007 ☐
3. 658 + 1,375 + 2,159 = 4,192 ☐
4. 3,159 + 2,556 + 1,282 = 6,997 ☐
5. 2,059 + 951 + 3,694 = 6,074 ☐
6. 3,852 + 2,159 + 2,753 = 8,674 ☐

F. Word puzzles

1. Aaron blew **2,135** bubbles and Zelda blew **2,865** bubbles. How many bubbles did they blow altogether? _____
2. A bubble factory made **1,600** cans of bubbles each day last week (5-day week). How many cans were made altogether? _____
3. Sam collects songs which he stores on his music players. Sam keeps his songs on two music players. He has **2,300** songs on one player. He has **300** more than that on the other player. How many songs has he altogether? _____
4. Clodagh has **6,000** songs altogether. She stores her songs on two music players. One player has **1,000** more songs than the other player. How many songs are on each player? _____

Test yourself!

1.
   $$4573 + 2818$$

   ☐ 6,381   ☐ 7,391
   ☐ 6,391   ☐ none of these

2.
   $$2164$$
   $$2587$$
   $$+ 1291$$

   ☐ 5,832   ☐ 5,834
   ☐ 6,042   ☐ none of these

3. 6,032 + 276 + 2,775 =

   ☐ 8,973   ☐ 8,978
   ☐ 983   ☐ none of these

4. Roisín is $9\frac{3}{4}$ years old. It is 3,561 days since she was born. Shane is 149 days older than Roisín. How many days old is Shane?

   _____

5. Use a calculator to add this list of five numbers:

   4,126 + 287 + 1,038 + 96 + 1,058 =

   _____

6. A dictionary has two parts. Part 1 has 984 pages. Part 2 has 112 pages more than Part 1. How many pages are there altogether?

   _____

7. Complete the magic square.

	4		7
8	9	13	6
8			
	5		9

8. Complete the magic square.

22			6
		13	
7	18	2	21
		16	9

9. Estimate:

   1,860 + 2,199 =

   ☐ 3,000   ☐ 4,000
   ☐ 5,000   ☐ 2,000

10. A newsagent sold 1,560 magazines in May. The number of magazines sold increased by 180 in June. How many magazines were sold altogether during the two months? _____

rough work

rough work

TOPIC 3 Time

A. Warm up!

1. What time is shown on each clock face?

(a) 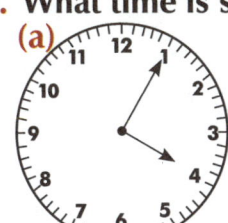 (b)  (c) 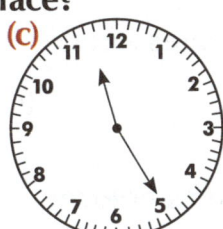 (d) 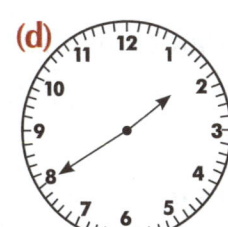 (e)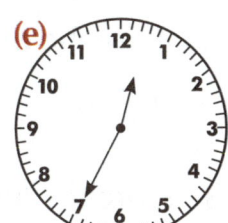

_____   _____   _____   _____   _____

2. Draw hands to show the following times.

(a) 10 past 5   (b) 20 to 11   (c) $\frac{1}{4}$ past 10   (d) $\frac{1}{4}$ to 10   (e) $\frac{1}{2}$ past 3

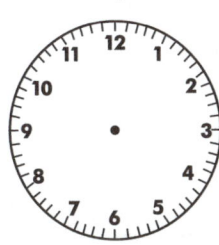 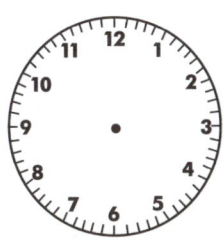 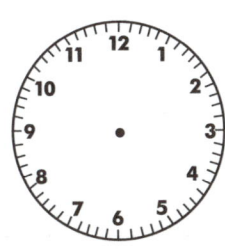 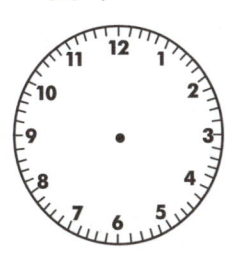 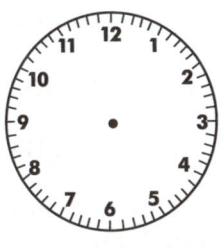

B. In your mathematical opinion

How long might it take you to:

1. do your homework _____

2. tidy your room _____

3. walk to school _____

C. Calendar puzzles

1. The month of April has 30 days. If 26th April is a Friday. What day is 1st May? _____

2. There are 24 hours in one day. How many hours are in $2\frac{1}{2}$ days? _____

3. A family arrived at their holiday home on 28th July and left on 8th August. How many nights did they sleep there? _____

D. Digital time

1. Show the following in digital time.

   (a) 23 mins past 7   (b) 10 to 11   (c) 16 mins to 4   (d) 27 mins to 3

2. Write the time that comes 12 minutes after:

   (a) 7:10 _____   (b) 11:45 _____   (c) 3:33 _____   (d) 7:52 _____

3. Write the time that comes 9 minutes before:

   (a) 6:00 _____   (b) 10:42 _____   (c) 2:22 _____   (d) 12:08 _____

E. To and past

Complete the following. e.g. 20 minutes to 9 is the same as 40 past 8.

1. 10 minutes to 9 is the same as _____.
2. 10 minutes to 7 is the same as _____.
3. 15 minutes to 2 is the same as _____.
4. 11 minutes to 5 is the same as _____.
5. _____ is the same as 44 minutes past 6.
6. _____ is the same as 53 minutes past 12.
7. _____ is the same as 39 minutes past 1.
8. _____ is the same as 44 minutes past 6.

F. Word puzzles

1. The **5th January** is a Tuesday. How many Thursdays are there in the month of January? _____
2. A game of hurling began at **11:30am** and ended at **12:50pm**. There was a 10-minute break in the middle. How long was each half? _____
3. How many times will the digit **'2'** appear on a digital clock between **3 o'clock** and **4 o'clock**? _____

12 Planet Maths Activity Book • 4th Class

Test yourself!

1. Write the time shown on the clock.

_____

2. Draw hands on the clock to show 2:52.

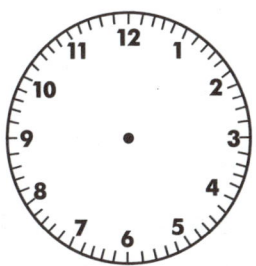

3. Write 27 minutes past 8 in digital time.

_____

4. Write 7:43 in a different way.

_____

5. $\frac{1}{4}$ past 6 = _____ in digital time

6. Do you eat your breakfast in the am or pm?

_____

7. What time comes 12 minutes after $\frac{1}{4}$ past 1?

☐ 3 minutes past 1
☐ $\frac{1}{2}$ past 1
☐ 27 minutes past 1
☐ 12 minutes to 2

8. What time comes 8 minutes before 10 to 9?

☐ 2 minutes to 9
☐ 20 to 9
☐ 18 minutes past 9
☐ none of these

9. What time comes $\frac{1}{4}$ of an hour after 4:56?

☐ 5:11 ☐ 4:41
☐ 4:31 ☐ none of these

10. A movie on TV began at 7:30 pm and ended at 9:20 pm. There were 4 breaks for advertisements, each lasting 3 minutes. How long was the movie?

_____

TOPIC 4 Lines and Angles

A. Warm up!

1. Colour the following.

  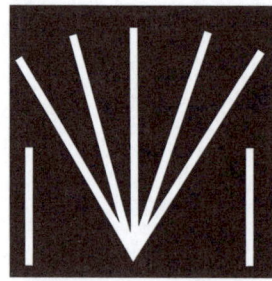 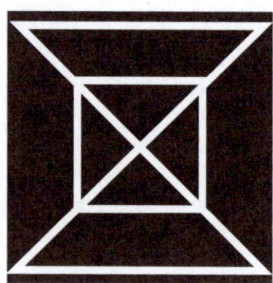

(a) The parallel lines (b) Lines that are perpendicular to the green line (c) The vertical lines (d) The horizontal lines

2. (a)

How many lines are vertical? _____

(b)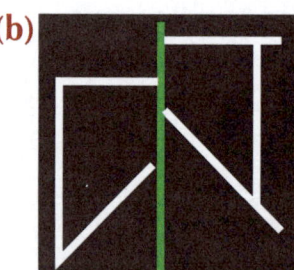

Colour the lines that are oblique to the green line.

(c)

Colour the diagonals of the rectangles.

(d)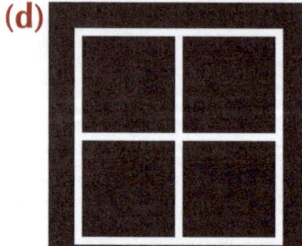

Colour the lines that are both parallel and horizontal.

B. In your mathematical opinion

Where do you think the bubble should be in each spirit level? Draw it.

1.

2.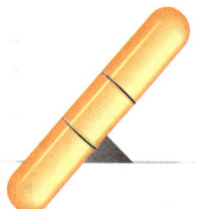

3.

C. How many?

1. How many of these can you see in the diagram?

   (a) right angles _____

   (b) acute angles _____

   (c) obtuse angles _____

2. Can you see any sets of parallel lines? _____

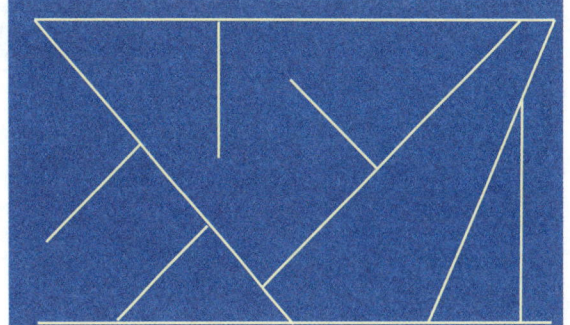

D. True or false?

1. Horizontal lines are perpendicular to vertical lines.   ☐ true ☐ false
2. A rectangle has 4 diagonals.   ☐ true ☐ false
3. Oblique lines are usually vertical.   ☐ true ☐ false
4. You are in a vertical position when you are asleep in bed.   ☐ true ☐ false
5. The rails on railway lines are an example of parallel lines.   ☐ true ☐ false

E. Puzzles

1. (a) Write the name of something that is usually vertical. _____

   (b) Write the name of something that is usually horizontal. _____

2. Jane was facing north-east. What direction will she face if she turns anti-clockwise through a right angle? _____

3. **Circle the correct answer.**

   (a) Line A runs from north to south. Line B runs from east to west. Therefore lines A and B are (vertical / perpendicular / parallel).

   (b) Line C runs from north to south. Line D runs from south-east to north-west. Therefore lines C and D are (parallel / perpendicular / oblique).

   (c) The hands of a clock move in a (clockwise / anti-clockwise) direction.

   (d) Ceilings and walls usually meet to form a (acute / right / obtuse / straight) angle.

Test yourself!

1. Draw arrows pointing to the horizontal lines.

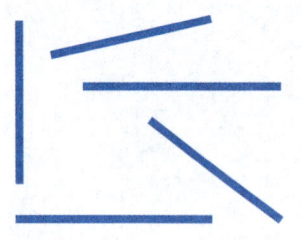

2. Draw arrows pointing to the parallel lines.

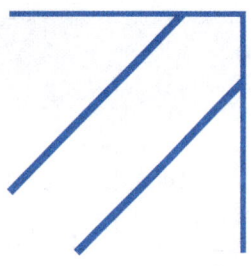

3. Draw arrows pointing to the blue lines that are oblique to the red line.

4. Tommy was facing north. He turned clockwise and now faces south-east. Through what type of angle has he turned?
   ☐ acute   ☐ right
   ☐ obtuse ☐ straight

5. Draw hands on the clock face to form an obtuse angle.

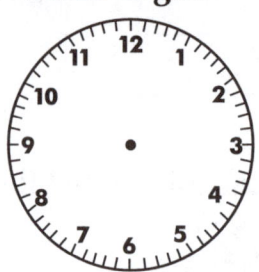

6. Draw a triangle that has one obtuse angle and two acute angles.

7. Is this angle: right, straight, obtuse, acute?

   _____

8. Which letter has a horizontal line? N or A?

   _____

9. True or false? Parallel lines never meet.

   _____

10. Draw a capital letter that has a right angle.

Topic 5: Subtraction

A. Warm up!

1. (a) 16 − 9 = _____ (b) 20 − 4 = _____ (c) 100 − 10 = _____
2. (a) 14 − 7 = _____ (b) 20 − 6 = _____ (c) 100 − 12 = _____
3. (a) 13 − 8 = _____ (b) 20 − 11 = _____ (c) 100 − 20 = _____
4. (a) 19 − 3 = _____ (b) 20 − 9 = _____ (c) 100 − 30 = _____
5. (a) 18 − 9 = _____ (b) 20 − 3 = _____ (c) 100 − 87 = _____
6. (a) 12 − 7 = _____ (b) 20 − 17 = _____ (c) 100 − 1 = _____
7. (a) 13 − 5 = _____ (b) 20 − 8 = _____ (c) 100 − 14 = _____

B. In your mathematical opinion

Which estimate is best? Circle it.

1. 8,126 − 2,891 =   5,000   6,000   7,000   8,000
2. 9,256 − 1,140 =   6,000   7,000   8,000   9,000
3. 7,863 − 4,444 =   1,000   2,000   3,000   4,000
4. 8,680 − 2,240 =   6,300   6,400   6,500   6,600

C. Calculate!

1.
(a) HTU 316 − 108
(b) HTU 426 − 194
(c) HTU 724 − 235
(d) HTU 924 − 238
(e) HTU 830 − 153
(f) HTU 704 − 126

2.
(a) ThHTU 4129 − 1046
(b) ThHTU 5282 − 2354
(c) ThHTU 6243 − 1169
(d) ThHTU 7147 − 2318
(e) ThHTU 8252 − 2466
(f) ThHTU 9111 − 2674

D. Operations

Should you add or subtract in these questions? (There's no need to work out the answers!)

1. Peter and Paul each have 2,250 cents. How many have they altogether? _____
2. Noreen has 3,600 beads. Nuala has 4,250 beads. How many more beads has Nuala than Noreen? _____
3. Adam has 1,800 cards. Nick has 600 cards more than Adam. How many have they altogether? _____
4. Sophia had 3,200 stamps. Sophia gave 850 stamps to Aoibhe and gave 750 stamps to Robyn. How many stamps has Sophia left? _____

E. Real-life maths

Jim has a stall at the farmers' market. He started on Monday with 1,200 pieces of fruit. During the week he sold the following amounts of fruit.

He sold:

Mon	Tues	Wed	Thurs	Fri
140 pieces	185 pieces	240 pieces	323 pieces	? pieces

1. How many pieces of fruit had he left on Friday? _____
2. Fruit does not stay fresh for too long. By Friday, 32 pieces of fruit could not be sold. How many pieces of fruit could Jim actually try to sell on Friday? _____

F. Word puzzles

1. There are **259** pages in Emma's book. She read **89** the first night and **102** the next night. How many pages has Emma left to read? _____
2. A bulb factory made **3,100** bulbs of which **235** were faulty. How many could be sold? _____
3. A theatre uses **1,000** bulbs. **432** of these are yellow, **146** are red and the rest are white. How many white bulbs are there? _____

Test yourself!

1.
   ```
   7826
   - 3254
   ```
   ☐ 4,632   ☐ 4,572
   ☐ 4,672   ☐ none of these

2.
   ```
   8406
   - 2138
   ```
   ☐ 6,332   ☐ 6,368
   ☐ 6,378   ☐ none of these

3.
   ```
   9003
   - 2185
   ```
   ☐ 6,818   ☐ 6,928
   ☐ 7,182   ☐ none of these

4. A man won a prize of €2,500. He spent €875 on a holiday. How much of the prize money was left?

   _____

5. A ship set out with 1,183 passengers. 250 more passengers came aboard the ship at the first port. How many passengers were then on the ship?

   _____

rough work

6. There were 1,600 people on a train. 134 got off at the first stop, 278 got off at the second stop. How many people were left on the train?

   _____

7. Professor Yeats has read 1,111 pages of a book with 2,000 pages. Professor Shaw has read 999 pages of the same book. How many more pages has Professor Yeats read than Professor Shaw?

   _____

Use a calculator to answer these three questions. Then add your three answers.

8. $5,126 - 2,257 =$

   _____

9. $4,149 - 3,380 =$

   _____

10. $9,006 - 7,159 =$

    _____

    Total = _____

rough work

TOPIC 6 Fractions

A. Warm up!

1. Colour.

(a) 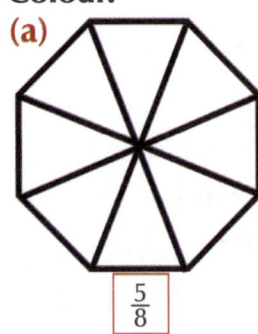 $\frac{5}{8}$

(b)  $\frac{7}{10}$

(c)  $\frac{3}{5}$

(d)  $\frac{7}{8}$

2. (a) 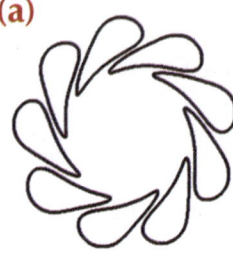 $\frac{4}{9}$

(b) 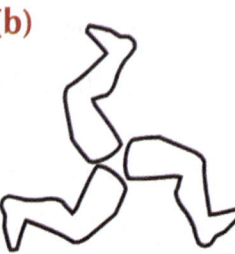 $\frac{2}{3}$

(c) 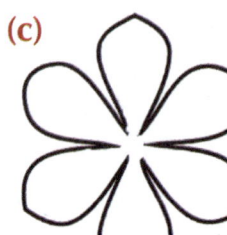 $\frac{5}{6}$

(d) 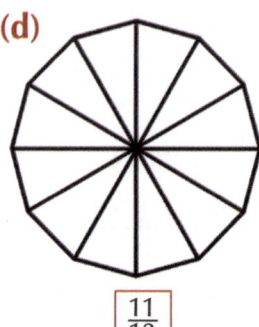 $\frac{11}{12}$

B. In your mathematical opinion

Without using a ruler, colour the following:

1. approx $\frac{4}{9}$

2. approx $\frac{11}{12}$

3. approx $\frac{1}{8}$

C. Calculate!

Find another fraction with the same value as the following.

1. $\frac{2}{4}$ = _____ 2. $\frac{2}{6}$ = _____ 3. $\frac{6}{8}$ = _____ 4. $\frac{2}{8}$ = _____ 5. $\frac{2}{2}$ = _____

D. Fill in the blanks

1. $\frac{1}{2}$ = half
2. $\frac{1}{4}$ = q _ _ _ _ _ _
3. $\frac{1}{6}$ = s _ _ _ _
4. $\frac{1}{9}$ = n _ _ _ _
5. $\frac{1}{3}$ = t h _ _ _
6. $\frac{1}{5}$ = f _ _ _ _
7. $\frac{1}{8}$ = e _ _ _ _ _
8. $\frac{1}{10}$ = t _ _ _ _

E. Real-life maths

Let's race!

1. Draw fences at:

   $\frac{1}{4}, \frac{1}{3}, \frac{1}{2}$ and $\frac{11}{12}$

2. Draw fences at:

   $\frac{1}{10}, \frac{1}{5}, \frac{1}{2}$ and $\frac{9}{10}$

3. Draw fences at:

   $\frac{1}{8}, \frac{1}{2}, \frac{3}{4}$ and $\frac{7}{8}$

F. Puzzles

1. Circle the fraction in each set that is closest in value to 1 unit.

Set A	Set B	Set C	Set D	Set E	Set F	Set G
$\frac{5}{8}$	$\frac{9}{10}$	$\frac{1}{3}$	$\frac{7}{12}$	$\frac{1}{5}$	$1\frac{4}{5}$	$1\frac{3}{10}$
$\frac{6}{8}$	$\frac{8}{10}$	$\frac{1}{2}$	$\frac{11}{12}$	$\frac{1}{10}$	$1\frac{3}{5}$	$\frac{3}{10}$
$\frac{7}{8}$	$\frac{7}{10}$	$\frac{1}{4}$	$\frac{9}{12}$	$\frac{2}{5}$	$1\frac{2}{5}$	$\frac{9}{10}$

2. A Christmas tree that was 12m high was too tall for the local hall. The ceiling was only 9m high. By what fraction did the height of the tree need to be reduced so that it would fit? _ _ _ _ _ _

3. Write half of each of the following.

   (a) $\frac{1}{2}$ _ _ _ _ _
   (b) $\frac{1}{4}$ _ _ _ _ _
   (c) $\frac{1}{6}$ _ _ _ _ _
   (d) $\frac{1}{3}$ _ _ _ _ _
   (e) $\frac{1}{5}$ _ _ _ _ _
   (f) $1\frac{1}{2}$ _ _ _ _ _

Test yourself!

1. Colour $\frac{5}{8}$ of the circle.

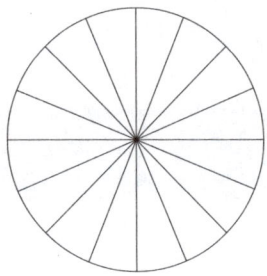

2. Colour all but $\frac{1}{12}$ of the circle.

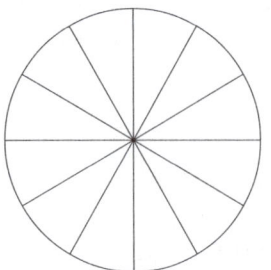

3. Write these fractions in order. Start with the smallest:

   $\frac{7}{9}$, $\frac{1}{12}$, $\frac{1}{3}$, $\frac{1}{9}$

   ___, ___, ___, ___,

4. Which fraction is bigger?

   $\frac{1}{9}$ or $\frac{1}{5}$ _____

5. Which fraction is smaller?

   $\frac{3}{8}$ or $\frac{1}{2}$ _____

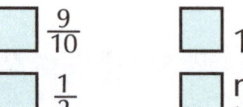

6. Which has the same value as $\frac{10}{10}$?

   ☐ $\frac{9}{10}$ ☐ 1 unit
   ☐ $\frac{1}{2}$ ☐ none of these

7. Which has the same value as $\frac{1}{2}$?

   ☐ $\frac{6}{12}$ ☐ $\frac{3}{4}$
   ☐ $\frac{9}{12}$ ☐ none of these

8. Which has the same value as $\frac{2}{3}$?

   ☐ $\frac{8}{9}$ ☐ $\frac{5}{6}$
   ☐ $\frac{12}{12}$ ☐ none of these

9. What fraction is one eighth less than one unit?

   _____

10. Write a fraction that has the same value as $\frac{8}{10}$.

    _____

Topic 7 Graphs

A. Warm up!

Kim loves to visit the airport and watch take-off and landing. The table below is a record of the aircraft she saw.

(a) In your copy, show the number of each aircraft Kim saw using a tally.

(b) In your copy, draw a bar graph to display this data.

Boeing 737	Cessna 172	Airbus A320	Cessna 172	Lear Jet	Helicopter
Helicopter	Boeing 737	Airbus A320	Cessna 172	Airbus A320	Lear Jet
Lear Jet	Helicopter	Boeing 737	Boeing 737	Helicopter	Boeing 737
Lear Jet	Helicopter	Helicopter	Cessna 172	Airbus A320	Boeing 737
Boeing 737	Helicopter	Boeing 737	Boeing 737	Airbus A320	Cessna 172

B. Calculate!

1. **This chart shows how many aircraft took off from its main runway during the week.**

   (a) How many aircraft took off on Monday? ____
   (b) On which day was the runway most busy? ____
   (c) On which day was the runway least busy? ____
   (d) How many aircraft took off at the weekend? ____
   (e) How many aircraft took off on weekdays? ____

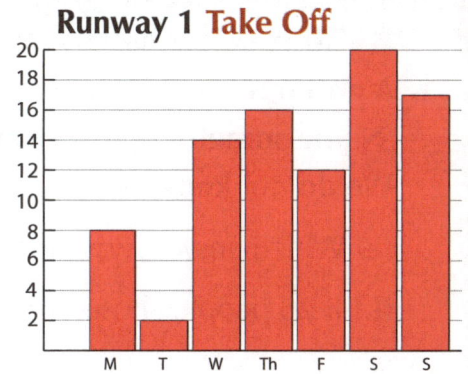

2. **This chart shows the number of aircraft landing.**

   (a) Which day was least busy? ____
   (b) How many planes landed on Thursday? ____
   (c) How many planes landed from Friday to Sunday? ____
   (d) How many more planes landed on Monday than on Tuesday? ____

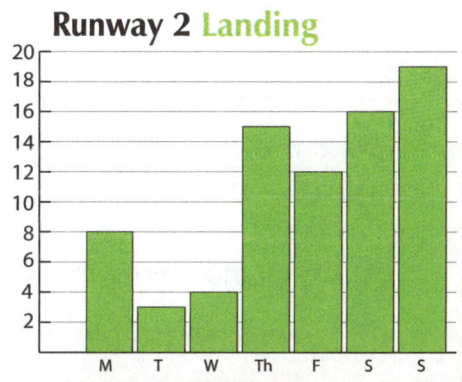

C. Real life maths

1. People at an airport were asked: 'What do you like most about airports and planes?' Record their answers on a bar chart.

taking off	18
watching planes	14
landing	5
excitement	20
airport shopping	12
meeting friends	2

D. Puzzles

1. A group of people were asked:
   'Name something that comes in pairs.'
   We do not know how many people were surveyed.

   (a) Which answer was most popular? _____

   (b) If 20 people chose 'glasses', how many people chose 'scissors'? _____

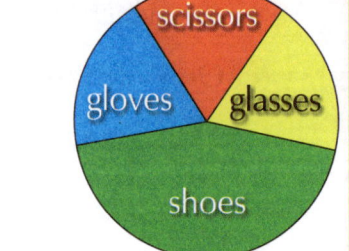

2. A group of people were asked to name somewhere you would find a pen. Their answers are given in the table below.

pencil case	28
drawer	16
car	4
jacket pocket	8
shirt pocket	8

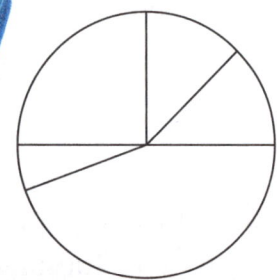

(a) Label and colour the pie chart to show these answers.

(b) How many people were surveyed? _____

Test yourself!

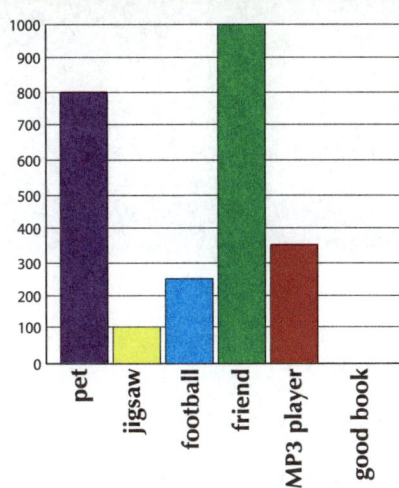

3,000 people were asked: 'If you were stuck on a desert island with enough food and water to last a month, what would you most like to have with you to keep you entertained?'

1. How many people chose 'football'? _____

2. Which answer was most popular? _____

3. How many more people chose 'pet' than 'MP3 player'? _____

4. Draw the missing bar on the graph for the number who chose 'good book'.

5. What is a circular graph called?
_____

36 children were asked to say what they usually did with their pocket money. The results are given in the pie chart.

6. How many said, 'buy sweets'?
_____

7. How many said, 'save'?
_____

8. What fraction said they buy comics?
_____

There are some mistakes in the graph below. Find 2 of them.

9. _____

10. _____

TOPIC 8 Multiplication

A. Warm up!

1. (a) 8 x 9 = _____   (b) 4 x 9 = _____   (c) 7 x 9 = _____
2. (a) 2 x 9 = _____   (b) 8 x 6 = _____   (c) 8 x 2 = _____
3. (a) 7 x 8 = _____   (b) 7 x 6 = _____   (c) 7 x 5 = _____
4. (a) 6 x 9 = _____   (b) 5 x 9 = _____   (c) 8 x 9 = _____
5. (a) 3 x 9 = _____   (b) 8 x 5 = _____   (c) 6 x 6 = _____

B. Calculate!

1. (a) 43 x 7   (b) 84 x 6   (c) 93 x 4   (d) 75 x 9   (e) 36 x 8

   (f) 86 x 7   (g) 62 x 5   (h) 48 x 3   (i) 91 x 8   (j) 74 x 6

2. Do the part inside the brackets first.
   (a) (4 x 2) x 3 and 4 x (2 x 3) = _____
   (b) (5 x 4) x 2 and 5 x (4 x 2) = _____
   (c) (5 x 3) x 2 and 5 x (3 x 2) = _____
   (d) (3 x 4) x 5 and 3 x (4 x 5) = _____

3. Leave the 10 times until last.
   (a) 10 x 8 x 2 = _____
   (b) 10 x 6 x 4 = _____
   (c) 10 x 3 x 5 = _____
   (d) 10 x 7 x 9 = _____
   (e) 8 x 7 x 10 = _____
   (f) 7 x 7 x 10 = _____
   (g) 6 x 9 x 10 = _____
   (h) 6 x 5 x 10 = _____
   (i) 9 x 10 x 8 = _____
   (j) 3 x 10 x 7 = _____

C. Operators

There is no need to work out the answers. Simply decide whether you should +, -, x or ÷.

1. Ava has 8 boxes, each with 25 beads. How many beads has she altogether? _____
2. Ben counted 160 children coming into the school hall of which 75 were boys. How many girls came into the hall? _____
3. Mia spotted 14 butterflies in the garden on Friday. She saw 8 more than that on Saturday. How many butterflies did she see on Saturday? _____
4. Robert has 44 minibeasts, shared equally among 4 containers. How many minibeasts are in each container? _____

D. Multiplying by 10

1. (a) 10 x | H | T | U |
   |---|---|---|
   | | 4 | 8 |
   = | H | T | U |

   (b) 10 x | H | T | U |
   |---|---|---|
   | | 9 | 0 |
   = | H | T | U |

2. (a) 10 x | H | T | U |
   |---|---|---|
   | | 5 | 9 |
   = | H | T | U |

   (b) 10 x | H | T | U |
   |---|---|---|
   | | 8 | 7 |
   = | H | T | U |

3. (a) 10 x | H | T | U |
   |---|---|---|
   | | 7 | 3 |
   = | H | T | U |

   (b) 10 x | H | T | U |
   |---|---|---|
   | | 5 | 8 |
   = | H | T | U |

E. Stretch the snake!

Draw Sammy 3 times as long as he is now. Draw Slim 4 times as long as he is now. Draw Stretch 6 times as long as he is now. Each snake is 6 squares long.

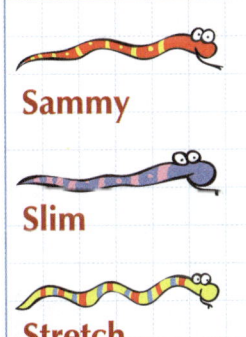

Sammy

Slim

Stretch

Test yourself!

1. 267
   x 4

2. 518
   x 9

3. It takes Tim 5 minutes to copy 46 pages. How many pages will he copy in 30 minutes?

4. How long does it take Charlie to swim 10 lengths of the pool if it takes him 48 seconds to swim one length?

5. How many players attended the basketball tournament if there were 35 teams? 14 teams brought 7 players and the other teams brought 8 players.

rough work

6. A barber was open for business 256 days last year. He gave 8 haircuts a day. How many haircuts did he give last year?

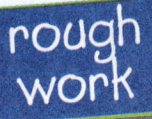

You must get all three sums right in each question to get a point.

7. (a) 12 x 1 = _____
   (b) 6 x 9 = _____
   (c) 3 x 8 = _____

8. (a) 6 x 2 = _____
   (b) 9 x 3 = _____
   (c) 7 x 8 = _____

9. (a) 6 x 7 = _____
   (b) 8 x 1 = _____
   (c) 12 x 0 = _____

10. (a) 8 x 8 = _____
    (b) 7 x 9 = _____
    (c) 6 x 10 = _____

rough work

TOPIC 9 Division

A. Warm up!

1. (a) 24 ÷ 3 = ____ (b) 55 ÷ 5 = ____ (c) 132 ÷ 12 = ____
2. (b) 35 ÷ 7 = ____ (b) 72 ÷ 8 = ____ (c) 4 ÷ 4 = ____
3. (c) 35 ÷ 5 = ____ (b) 36 ÷ 4 = ____ (c) 21 ÷ 3 = ____
4. (d) 81 ÷ 9 = ____ (b) 54 ÷ 6 = ____ (c) 42 ÷ 7 = ____
5. (e) 72 ÷ 6 = ____ (b) 63 ÷ 9 = ____ (c) 45 ÷ 9 = ____

B. In your mathematical opinion

1. €20 is shared between Harry and Lily. How much money did each person receive?
   _____

2. €20 is shared equally between Nathan and Saoirse. How much money did each person receive? _____

3. There was only one correct answer to question 2. Question 1 has many correct answers. Why do you think this is so?
   _____

C. Calculate!

1. (a) 5 ⟌ 95   (b) 4 ⟌ 72   (c) 8 ⟌ 96   (d) 3 ⟌ 84   (e) 2 ⟌ 98

2. (a) Share 60 marbles fairly among 12 children. _____
   (b) Share 94 beads fairly between 2 children. _____
   (c) Share 110 sweets fairly among 10 children. _____

3. What numbers can always be divided evenly by 2?
   ☐ big numbers   ☐ small numbers
   ☐ even numbers ☐ odd numbers

D. Sharing repeated subtraction

There is no need to answer the question – simply decide if it is sharing or repeated subtraction.

1. Divide 100 sweets equally among 4 children. _____
2. A lift can carry 5 people at a time. How many trips will it make to carry 100 people? _____
3. How many crates will I need to carry 200 boxes, if a crate can hold 10 boxes? _____
4. 3 medals are awarded in each event in a swimming gala. How many medals will be given out if there are 21 events? _____
5. A deck of cards is dealt one at a time among 5 players. How many cards will each person receive? _____

E. Remainders

1. (a) 17 ÷ 2 = _____ (b) 56 ÷ 6 = _____ (c) 5 ÷ 7 = _____
2. (a) 39 ÷ 5 = _____ (b) 20 ÷ 3 = _____ (c) 35 ÷ 4 = _____
3. (a) 41 ÷ 7 = _____ (b) 57 ÷ 9 = _____ (c) 70 ÷ 8 = _____
4. (a) 6 ÷ 8 = _____ (b) 42 ÷ 5 = _____ (c) 80 ÷ 9 = _____
5. (a) 19 ÷ 3 = _____ (b) 21 ÷ 2 = _____ (c) 31 ÷ 3 = _____
6. (a) 34 ÷ 9 = _____ (b) 50 ÷ 8 = _____ (c) 31 ÷ 5 = _____
7. (a) 17 ÷ 4 = _____ (b) 78 ÷ 7 = _____ (c) 23 ÷ 2 = _____
8. (a) 73 ÷ 6 = _____ (b) 22 ÷ 4 = _____ (c) 53 ÷ 6 = _____
9. (a) 6 ⟌99 (b) 2 ⟌93 (c) 4 ⟌83 (d) 5 ⟌91 (e) 7 ⟌96

F. Puzzles

In the following questions share the items as fairly as possible. Leave no one out.

1. Share 20 CDs among 3 children. _____
2. Share 30 books as fairly as possible among 4 children. _____
3. Share 25 apples as fairly as possible among 6 children. _____

Test yourself!

In questions 1 and 2 you must get all four sums in each question right to get a point.

1. (a) 24 ÷ 8 = _____
   (b) 22 ÷ 2 = _____
   (c) 27 ÷ 3 = _____
   (d) 35 ÷ 5 = _____

2. (a) 23 ÷ 9 = _____
   (b) 37 ÷ 4 = _____
   (c) 40 ÷ 6 = _____
   (d) 62 ÷ 12 = _____

3. Share 80c among 7 people giving each person the same amount. How much is left over?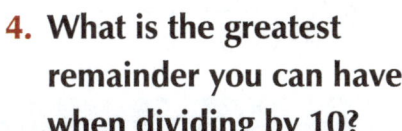

   _____

4. What is the greatest remainder you can have when dividing by 10?

   _____

5. How many trays will I need to hold 52 eggs if each tray holds 6 eggs? Write the number sentence.

   ☐ ÷ ☐ = ☐

6. Fred has 85 bottles. How many trips will Fred need to make to the bottle bank if he can carry ten bottles at a time?

   _____

7. Share 39c among 4 people as fairly as possible.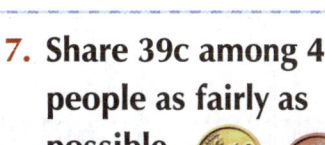

   _____

8. $\frac{1}{4}$ of 32 =

   ☐ 8   ☐ 6
   ☐ 7   ☐ 9

9. What is the remainder when you divide 7 into 60?

   ☐ 8   ☐ 4
   ☐ 3   ☐ none of these

10. A number is divided by 6 and the remainder is 4. What might the number be?

    ☐ 20   ☐ 24
    ☐ 16   ☐ none of these

TOPIC 10 Decimal Numbers

A. Warm up!

1. Look at each jar of jelly beans. **Approximately** how full is each one? Answer as a decimal.

(a) _____ (b) _____ (c) _____ (d) _____ (e) _____ (f) _____ (g) _____ (h) _____

2. Show the decimal numbers on the hundred squares.

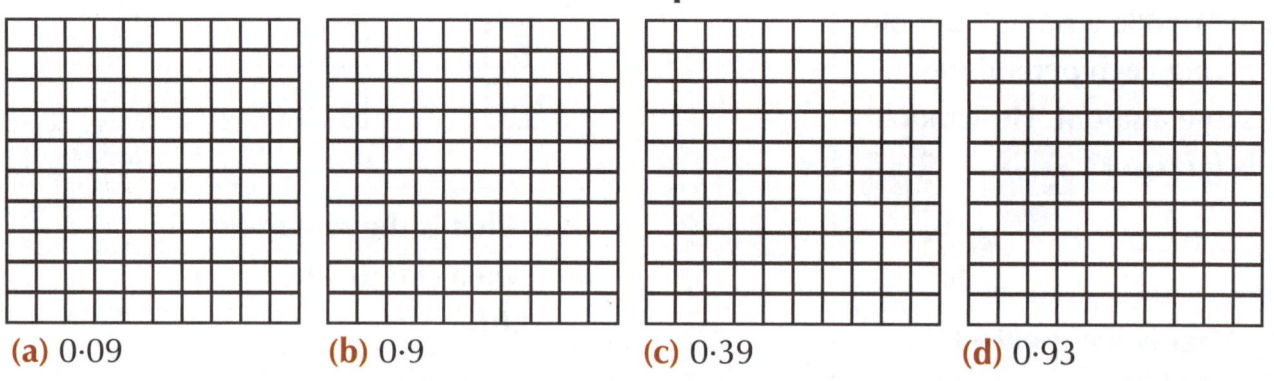

(a) 0·09   (b) 0·9   (c) 0·39   (d) 0·93

B. Calculate!

1. Change each fraction to a decimal number.

(a) $\frac{97}{100}$ = _____   (b) $\frac{83}{100}$ = _____   (c) $\frac{3}{10}$ = _____

(d) $\frac{7}{10}$ = _____   (e) $\frac{3}{4}$ = _____   (f) $\frac{11}{10}$ = _____

2. Change each decimal number to a fraction.

(a) 0·71 = _____   (b) 0·69 = _____   (c) 0·06 = _____

(d) 0·9 = _____   (e) 1·28 = _____   (f) 2·59 = _____

C. Number line

Fill in the empty boxes.

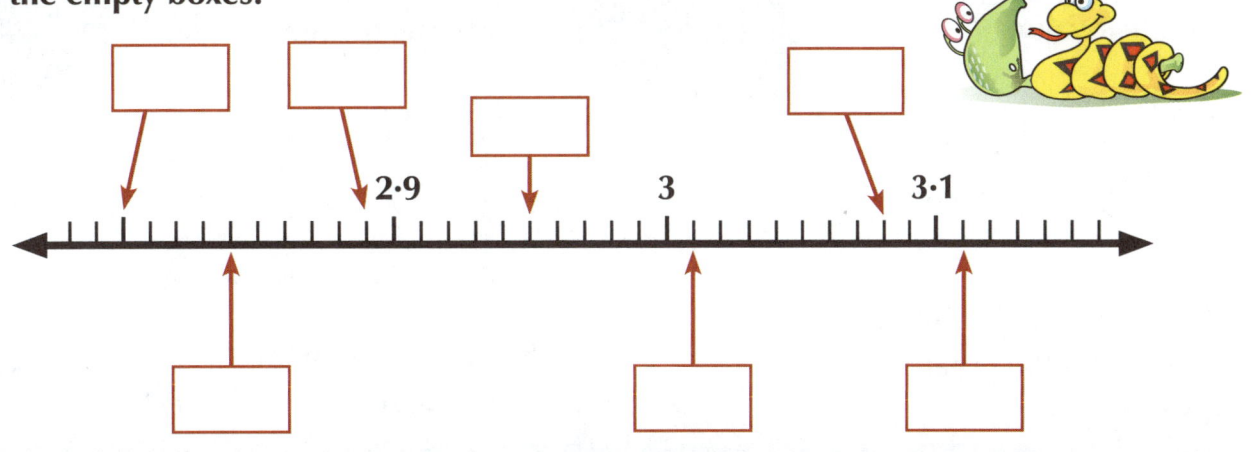

D. Real-life maths

Colour the fireworks to show the decimal number.

 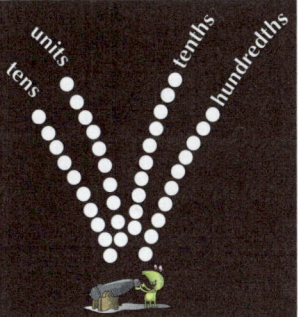 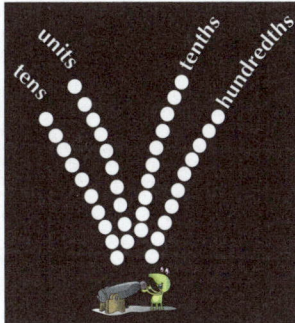 

1. 24·39   **2.** 82·16   **3.** 27·05   **4.** 30·08

E. Calculate!

1. How much more do you need to make 1 unit?

   (a) 0·97   (b) 0·02   (c) 0·56   (d) 0·18   (e) 0·2   (f) 0·6

   _____   _____   _____   _____   _____   _____

   (g) 0·84   (h) 0·37   (i) 0·42   (j) 0·03   (k) 0·14   (l) 0·99

   _____   _____   _____   _____   _____   _____

2. Oliver has read 0·4 of a book. Faye has read 0·04 of the same book.

   (a) Who has read more of the book? _____

   (b) How much more of the book has Oliver read than Faye? _____

Test yourself!

1. Which of these has the greatest value?

☐ 0·38   ☐ 0·8
☐ 0·83   ☐ 0·09

2. In which number has the numeral 4 the greatest value?

☐ 9·43   ☐ 2·14
☐ 0·34   ☐ 4·08

3. The number 2·06 is the same as:

☐ $2\frac{6}{100}$ ☐ $\frac{26}{100}$
☐ $2\frac{60}{100}$ ☐ none of these

4. Write $\frac{1}{4}$ as a decimal number.

_____

5. Write 1·2 as a fraction.

_____

6. True or false?

$\frac{1}{2} > 0·6$

☐ true   ☐ false

7. Draw rings on the abacus to show 51·08.

tens   units $\frac{1}{10}$ $\frac{1}{100}$

8. Which number lies between 1·95 and 2·05?

☐ 2·1   ☐ 2·11
☐ 1·9   ☐ 2

9. Which of these numbers is less than 1·11?

☐ 1·12   ☐ 1·01
☐ 1·21   ☐ 1·2

10. Which of these numbers lies to the right of 1·5 on the number line?

☐ 1·4   ☐ 1·05
☐ 0·9   ☐ none of these

TOPIC 11 Money

A. Warm up!

Make amounts of money using as few coins as possible. The first one is done for you.

	€2	€1	50c	20c	10c	5c	2c	1c
€4·91	2		1	2				1
€4·55								
€4·45								
€4·23								
€3·99								
€2·38								
€1·77								
€0·88								
€0·37								

B. Calculate!

1. What change should you get from €10 if you spend the following.

   (a) €8·00 _____   (b) €9·55 _____   (c) €7·56 _____   (d) €4·35 _____

2. Which has the greater value?

   (a) €1 coin **or** four 20c coins _____

   (b) €2 coin **or** five 50c coins _____

   (c) €5 note **or** three €2 coins _____

   (d) Four 20c coins **or** one 50c and seven 5c coins _____

3. Write the following as euro.

   (a) 432c = €_____   (b) 159c = €_____   (c) 288c = €_____   (d) 670c = €_____

4. How many €10 notes are there in the following?

   (a) €50 _____   (b) €20 _____   (c) €90 _____
   (d) €100 _____   (e) €150 _____   (f) €200 _____

5. How many €20 notes are there in the following?

   (a) €40 _____   (b) €80 _____   (c) €100 _____   (d) €140 _____

C. Real-life maths

An online shop sells baseball caps at the prices shown. You can have your own message printed on the cap.

baseball cap – white: €4·50
baseball cap – navy: €5·50
baseball cap – black: €6·50
LETTERING
plain: 20c per letter
gold: 25c per letter
No more than 20 letters.

1. How much would you pay for two white baseball caps, with no lettering? €_____

2. How much would you pay for two navy caps and one black baseball cap, with no lettering? €_____

3. How much would you pay for one white baseball cap with the word **Wizard** in plain lettering? €_____

4. How much would you pay for one navy baseball cap with the words **Little Genius** in gold lettering? €_____

5. How much would you pay for one black baseball cap with the words **Teacher's Pet** in gold lettering (you have to pay for the apostrophe)? €_____

6. Why do you think there is a notice: **No more than 20 letters**? _____

D. Word puzzles

1. An online photo shop charges **25c** for prints. There is a postage fee of **€1·50**. How much will you pay for 9 prints? €_____

2. A shopkeeper held a sale in which he cut his prices by half.
   (a) Emma bought a football before the sale and it cost her **€6·80**. How much would she have paid for the ball in the sale? €_____
   (b) Ryan bought a tennis racket for **€8·40** in the sale. What was the price of the racket before the sale? €_____

E. Puzzle

A pen costs **3 times** as much as a pencil.

How much is a pencil if 3 pens cost 99c? _____

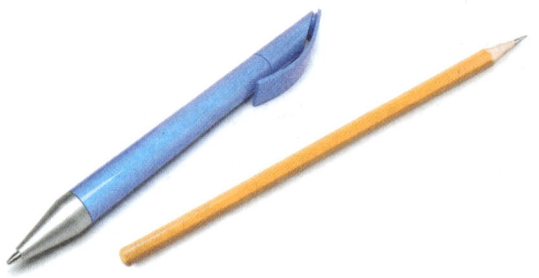

Test yourself!

1. How much will you have if you have two 50c coins, three 20c coins and four 10c coins?

   _____

2. €3·48
   + €4·59

3. €7·05
   − €2·28

4. €2·37
   × 6

5. 96c ÷ 4 = _____

6. Which of these has the same value as €5·05?

   ☐ 550c   ☐ 500c
   ☐ 505c   ☐ none of these

7. What change will you get from €5 if you spend €1·99?

   ☐ €2·01   ☐ €3·01
   ☐ €4·01   ☐ none of these

8. Which of these is the best value for money?

   ☐ 2 for 20c
   ☐ 3 for 33c
   ☐ 4 for 32c
   ☐ 5 for 45c

9. Andrew had €10. He bought a kite costing €5·99 and a roll of string costing €2·50. How much money has he left?

   _____

10. Ruby bought 2 colouring books, each costing €1·99, and a packet of crayons for €1·80. She has 22c left. How much did she have before she bought the items?

    _____

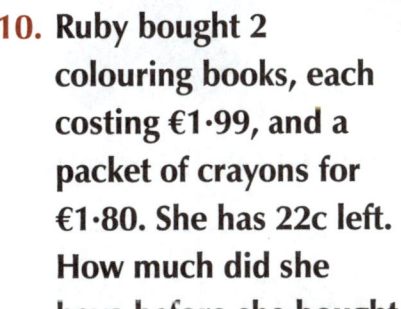

TOPIC 12 Symmetry

A. Warm up!

1. **Draw one or more lines of symmetry in each shape.**

2. **Draw the reflection in the mirror. The first one has been done for you.**

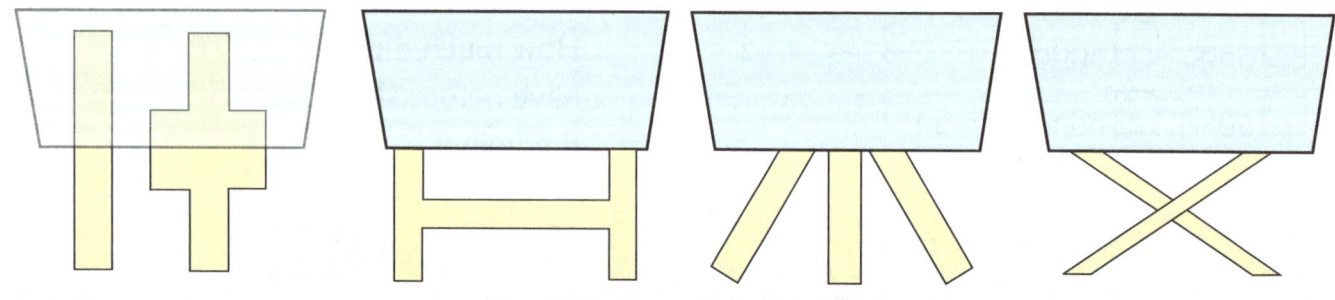

B. Try these

1. The vertical line in each kite is a line of symmetry.
   Complete the missing pattern on half of each kite.
   Colour the kites, keeping the colours symmetrical.

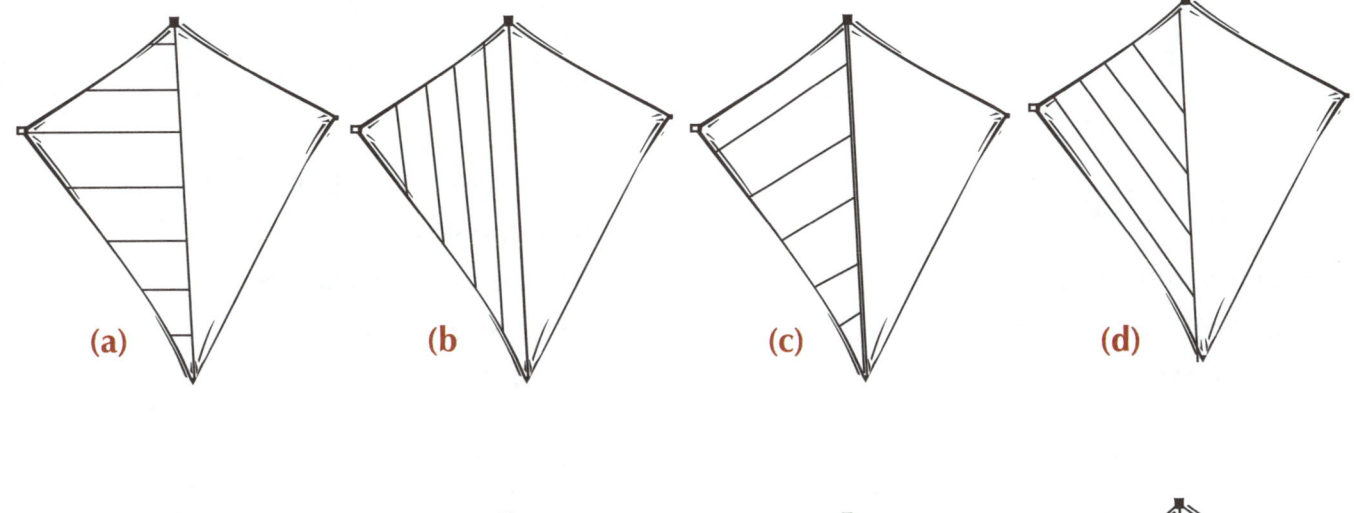

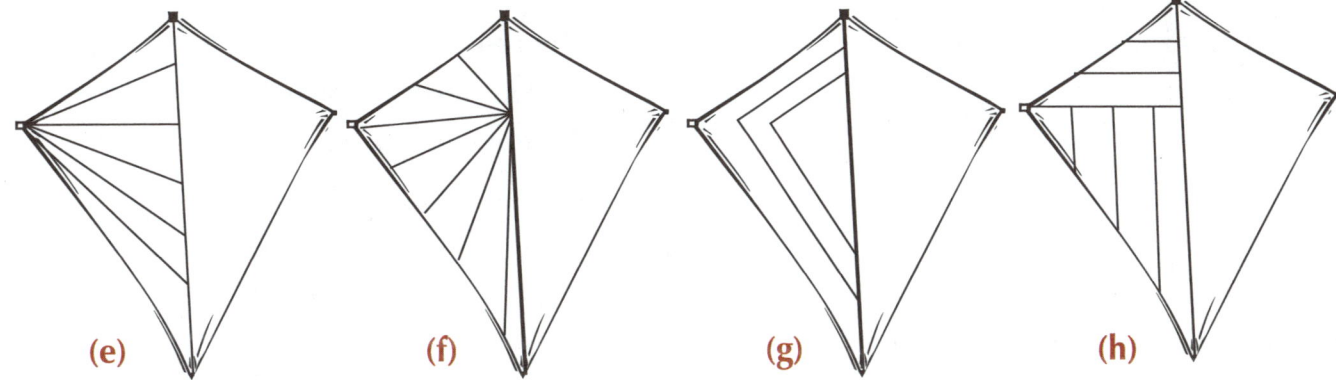

2. The pictures below have both a vertical and a horizontal line of symmetry.
   Colour the pictures, keeping the colours symmetrical.

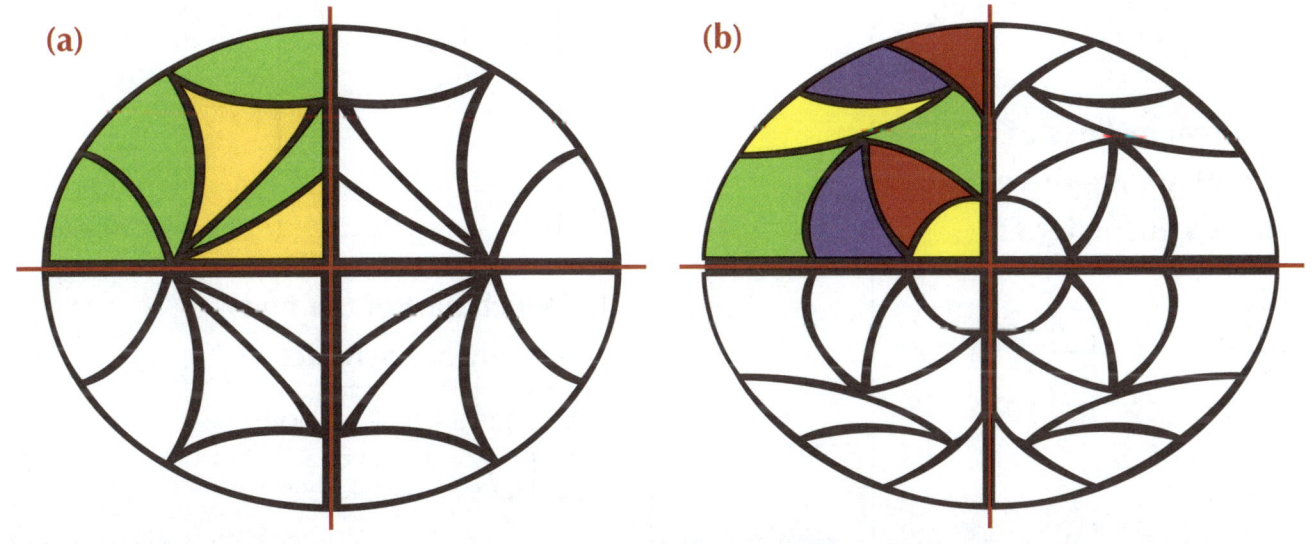

Test yourself!

1. Draw a line of symmetry in the picture of the rabbit.

2. Write a letter of the alphabet that has no line of symmetry.

   _____

3. Draw a shape that has a line of symmetry.

4. Choose a number between 1 and 9 that has both a horizontal line and a vertical line of symmetry.

   _____

5. How many lines of symmetry are there in a capital letter E?

   ☐ 0   ☐ 2
   ☐ 1   ☐ 10

6. How many lines of symmetry has a circle?

   ☐ 0   ☐ 2
   ☐ 1   ☐ many

7. What word, starting with the letter 'r', describes what you see when you look in a mirror?

   _____

8. The red lines are lines of symmetry. Complete the missing parts.

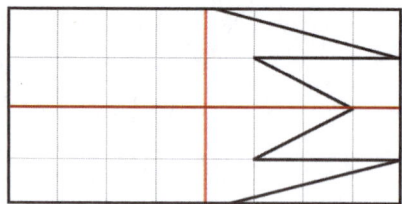

9.

10. Which part of the body usually has symmetry?

    ☐ hand   ☐ foot
    ☐ face   ☐ ear

40 Planet Maths Activity Book • 4th Class

Topic 13: Length

A. Warm up!

How many centimetres are there in the following?

1. (a) 2m = _____ cm (b) $8\frac{1}{4}$m = _____ cm (c) 7·16m = _____ cm
2. (a) 5m = _____ cm (b) $9\frac{3}{4}$m = _____ cm (c) 3·08m = _____ cm

B. In your mathematical opinion

1. **Estimate the heights of the following.**

   (a) your height _____
   (b) height of basketball net _____
   (c) your teacher's height _____
   (d) height of your classroom _____

2. **Estimate the following distances.**

   (a) from school to home _____
   (b) from where you sit in the classroom to the school gate _____

C. Calculate!

1. (a) 1·68m + 3·17m = _____   (b) 2·29m + 3·84m = _____
   (c) 4·63m + 2·87m = _____   (d) 2·6m + 2·06m = _____
2. (a) 6·38m − 2·19m = _____   (b) 7·26m − 2·14m = _____
   (c) 9·27m − 3·48m = _____   (d) 8·02m − 3·17m = _____
3. (a) 56cm ÷ 2 = _____   (b) 76cm ÷ 4 = _____
   (c) 95cm ÷ 5 = _____   (d) 98cm ÷ 7 = _____
4. (a) 23cm x 2 = _____   (b) 13cm x 3 = _____
   (c) 8cm x 5 = _____   (d) 30cm x 10 = _____

D. Estimate

1. Estimate the length of each line and then measure it. How close were your estimates? Work out the difference between your estimate and the actual length. Fill in the chart below.

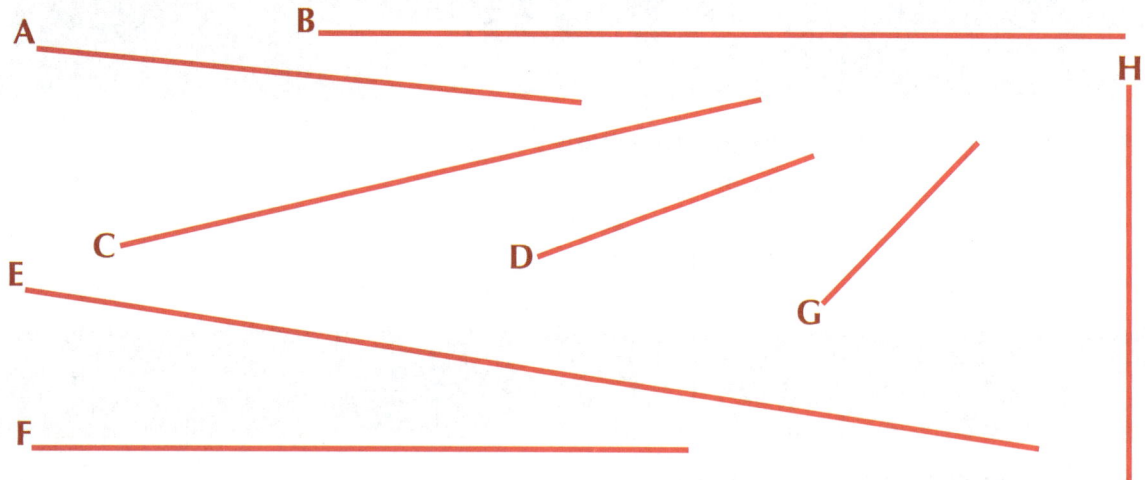

line	estimated length	actual length	difference
A			
B			
C			
D			

line	estimated length	actual length	difference
E			
F			
G			
H			

2. What is the length of each red line?

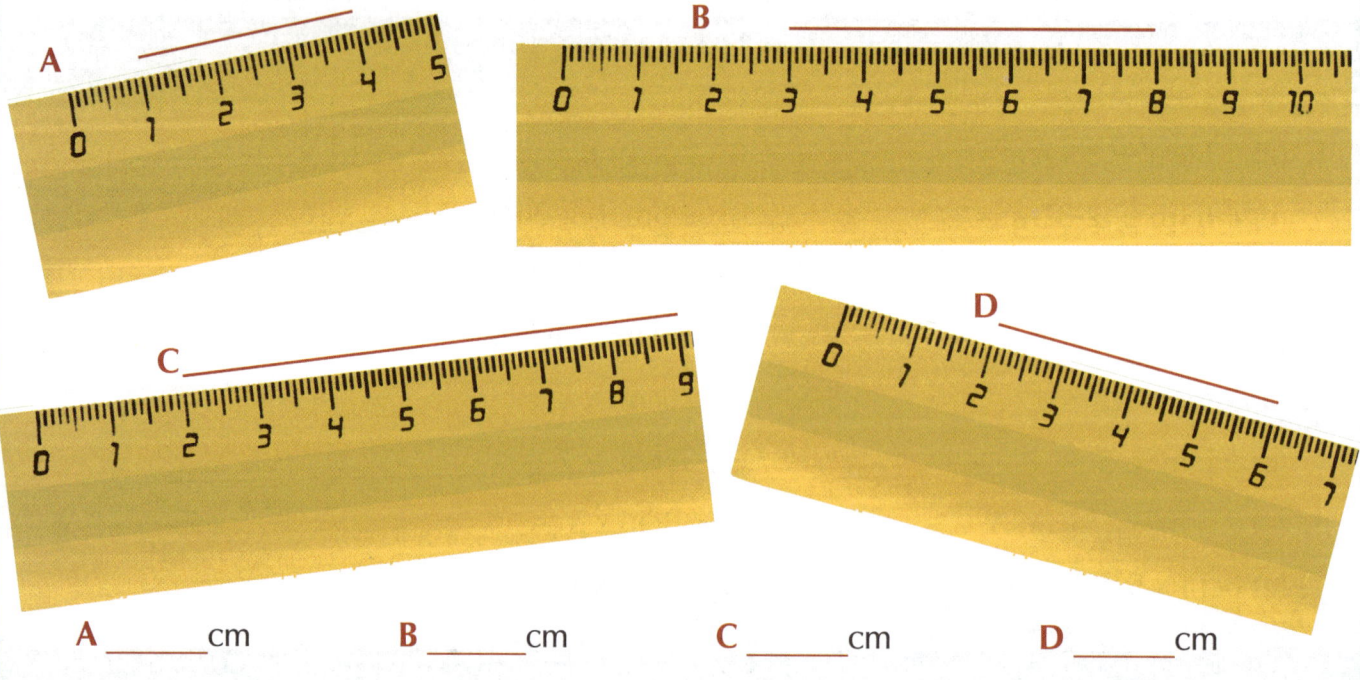

A _____ cm   B _____ cm   C _____ cm   D _____ cm

42 Planet Maths Activity Book • 4th Class

Test yourself!

1. The width of a doorway is most likely to be:
   - ☐ 30cm
   - ☐ 90cm
   - ☐ 30m
   - ☐ 9cm

2. Measure this line with your ruler.

   ─────────
   - ☐ 2cm
   - ☐ 3cm
   - ☐ $2\frac{1}{2}$ cm
   - ☐ $3\frac{1}{2}$ cm

3. 5m 9cm is the same as:
   - ☐ 5·9m
   - ☐ 5·90m
   - ☐ 5·09m
   - ☐ none of these

4.
   ```
         m
      4·26
     +2·58
   ```
   - ☐ 7·11m
   - ☐ 6·84m
   - ☐ 6·74m
   - ☐ 7·84m

5.
   ```
         m
      9·46
     −2·73
   ```
   - ☐ 6·73m
   - ☐ 7·33m
   - ☐ 6·33m
   - ☐ 6·27m

6. 8·04m − 3·28m =
   - ☐ 4·84m
   - ☐ 5·24m
   - ☐ 4·76m
   - ☐ none of these

7. The hockey club is 1·75km from Matt's home. The cinema is 0·85km from his home. How far does Matt walk if he walks to the hockey club, takes the bus home and then walks to the cinema and back?
   - ☐ 5·20km
   - ☐ 3·45km
   - ☐ 2·60km
   - ☐ none of these

8. A building has 5 storeys. Each one is $2\frac{1}{4}$m high. The roof is $3\frac{1}{2}$m high. The height of the building is:
   - ☐ 14·75m
   - ☐ 11·25m
   - ☐ 28·75m
   - ☐ none of these

9. It takes a centipede 4 minutes to walk 0·92m. How far does it walk in one minute?
   - ☐ 23m
   - ☐ 23cm
   - ☐ 368m
   - ☐ 368cm

10. A running track measures 400m. How far does Caoimhe run if she runs around the track $3\frac{1}{2}$ times?
    - ☐ 1·04km
    - ☐ 1km 40m
    - ☐ 1·40m
    - ☐ none of these

Topic 14: Long Multiplication

A. Warm up!

1. (a) 10 x 9 = _____ (b) 10 x 46 = _____ (c) 10 x 168 = _____
2. (a) 10 x 11 = _____ (b) 10 x 65 = _____ (c) 10 x 219 = _____
3. (a) 10 x 14 = _____ (b) 10 x 70 = _____ (c) 10 x 368 = _____
4. (a) 10 x 18 = _____ (b) 10 x 81 = _____ (c) 10 x 459 = _____
5. (a) 10 x 23 = _____ (b) 10 x 93 = _____ (c) 10 x 674 = _____

B. In your mathematical opinion

Four children were asked to multiply 79 by 68 and not one of them got the right answer. Can you figure out each child's mistake.

Andy _____
Emma _____
John _____
Evan _____

Andy	Emma	John	Evan
79	78	79	79
x 68	x 69	x 68	x 68
562	702	632	632
4740	4680	474	4740
5302	5382	1106	4372

C. Try these

1.
(a) 43 x 40
(b) 59 x 60
(c) 94 x 80
(d) 126 x 30
(e) 138 x 20
(f) 108 x 90

2. How many sweets are in 40 packets if each packet holds 16 sweets? _____

3. A newsagent stacked 60 magazines on top of one another. How many pages are in the stack altogether if each magazine has 32 pages? _____

4. How much does Mr Rich have if he has 360 €20 notes? _____

D. Calculate!

1.
(a) 49 × 37
(b) 86 × 53
(c) 94 × 71
(d) 28 × 98
(e) 46 × 27

2. (a) 53 × 19 = ____   (b) 25 × 33 = ____   (c) 67 × 82 = ____
(d) 64 × 16 = ____   (e) 38 × 45 = ____   (f) 74 × 67 = ____
(g) 82 × 18 = ____   (h) 41 × 53 = ____   (i) 87 × 40 = ____

E. Puzzles

1. A theatre with **86** seats was filled every night in January (**31** nights), except for one night when there were **5** empty seats. How many people altogether came to the theatre that month? ____

2. How many hours are there in the month of January? ____

3. **Place the letter above the correct answer to crack the code.**

Where do parrots go to star in films?

9,288	3,741	6,226	6,226	7,540	8,918	3,741	3,741	9,856

Y = 145 × 52 ____   D = 308 × 32 ____   P = 258 × 36 ____
L = 283 × 22 ____   W = 182 × 49 ____   O = 129 × 29 ____

F. Fill in the blank

What numbers belong in the blanks?

1. 128
    × 46
    ─────
    7 6 _
    5 1 2 0
    ─────
    5 8 8 8

2. 238
    × 34
    ─────
    9 _ 2
    7 1 4 0
    ─────
    8 0 9 2

3. 409
    × 17
    ─────
    2 8 6 3
    4 0 _ 0
    ─────
    6 9 5 3

4. 1 _ 7
    × 32
    ─────
    3 3 4
    5 0 1 0
    ─────
    5 3 4 4

5. 238
    × 2 _
    ─────
    9 5 2
    4 7 6 0
    ─────
    5 7 1 2

Test yourself!

Answer the sums below. You must get all 4 sums correct in each question to earn a point.

1. (a) 5 x 8 = _____
   (b) 9 x 9 = _____
   (c) 8 x 6 = _____
   (d) 7 x 9 = _____

2. (a) 10 x 14 = _____
   (b) 10 x 26 = _____
   (c) 10 x 35 = _____
   (d) 10 x 84 = _____

3. (a) 10 x 159 = _____
   (b) 10 x 246 = _____
   (c) 10 x 388 = _____
   (d) 10 x 893 = _____

4. 67
   X 40

   ☐ 268   ☐ 248
   ☐ 2,680   ☐ 2,480

5. 87
   x 56

   ☐ 4,532   ☐ 4,872
   ☐ 957   ☐ none of these

6. 183
   x 26

   ☐ 4,758   ☐ 3,348
   ☐ 1,464   ☐ none of these

rough work

7. Shauna asked her friends to sponsor her. Each of her 24 friends promised her 75c. How much did she collect?

   € _____

8. The 25 children in fourth class have been recycling. 14 of the children each put 24 old AA batteries in the recycling bin. Each of the other children brought 18 old AAA batteries to the bin. How many batteries did they recycle?

   _____

9. It takes 90 minutes for one shirt to dry on the line. Dad hung out 15 shirts. How long did it take them to dry?

   _____

10. Amy plants 18 tomato plants per tray. She plants 24 lettuce plants per tray. She sold 30 trays of tomatoes and 45 trays of lettuce. How many plants did she sell altogether?

    _____

rough work

46 Planet Maths Activity Book • 4th Class

Topic 15 Fractions 2

A. Warm up!

Colour $\frac{1}{4}$ of the dogs; $\frac{1}{5}$ of the foxes; $\frac{1}{8}$ of the cows.

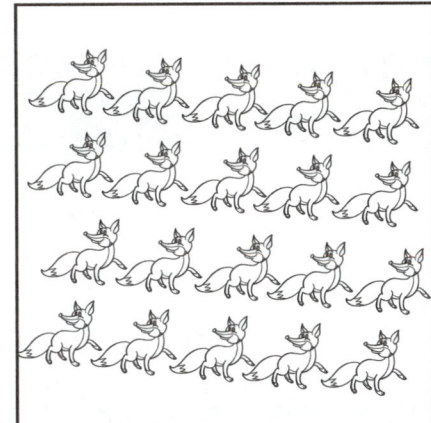

B. In your mathematical opinion

$\frac{1}{5}$ of one of the circles below is coloured yellow. Which one is it? _____

A   B   C

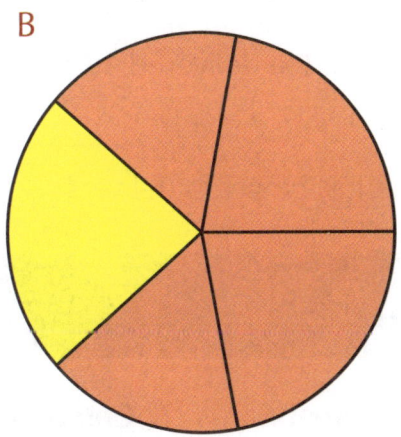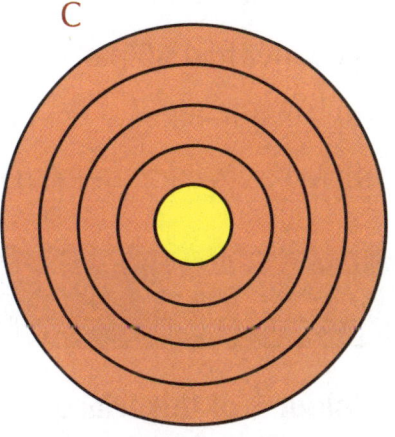

C. Calculate!

1. $\frac{1}{3}$ of 27 = _____
2. $\frac{1}{9}$ of 72 = _____
3. $\frac{1}{10}$ of 80 = _____
4. $\frac{1}{5}$ of 35 = _____
5. $\frac{1}{12}$ of 24 = _____
6. $\frac{1}{4}$ of 100 = _____

D. Multiple choice

1. $\frac{2}{5}$ of a number is 10. What is the number?
   ☐ 25
   ☐ 4
   ☐ 2
   ☐ none of these

2. $\frac{3}{4}$ of a number is 15. What is the number?
   ☐ 5
   ☐ 10
   ☐ 15
   ☐ none of these

3. $\frac{3}{8}$ of a number is 24. What is the number?
   ☐ 3
   ☐ 9
   ☐ 64
   ☐ none of these

E. Write the whole number if...

1. (a) $\frac{1}{2}$ of the number is 8 _____
   (b) $\frac{4}{9}$ of the number is 8 _____
2. (a) $\frac{2}{3}$ of the number is 8 _____
   (b) $\frac{2}{5}$ of the number is 20 _____
3. (a) $\frac{1}{6}$ of the number is 11 _____
   (b) $\frac{5}{8}$ of the number is 40 _____

F. Word puzzle

1. Sandra swam **one** length of a swimming pool which is **50m** long. She swam **5m** of this, underwater. What fraction did she swim underwater? _____
2. A climber carried a rucksack with **24kg** of gear. To make his load lighter he took out **8kg** and left it on the mountainside. What fraction of his gear did he take out? _____
3. A courier had **60** parcels to deliver. He delivered **12** of them this morning.
   (a) What fraction of the parcels did he deliver? _____
   (b) What fraction of the parcels has he yet to deliver? _____

G. Puzzle

1. Colour $\frac{1}{3}$ of this triangle red, $\frac{1}{3}$ green and $\frac{1}{3}$ blue.

2. Colour $\frac{1}{4}$ of this triangle red, $\frac{1}{4}$ green, $\frac{1}{4}$ blue and $\frac{1}{4}$ yellow.

Test yourself!

In questions 1 and 2 You must get all the 4 of the sums right to get a point.

1. (a) $\frac{1}{2}$ of 22 = _____
   (b) $\frac{1}{3}$ of 27 = _____
   (c) $\frac{1}{6}$ of 42 = _____
   (d) $\frac{1}{9}$ of 72 = _____

2. (a) $\frac{3}{4}$ of 20 = _____
   (b) $\frac{2}{5}$ of 35 = _____
   (c) $\frac{7}{8}$ of 24 = _____
   (d) $\frac{9}{10}$ of 80 = _____

3. Angie baked 42 buns, but $\frac{1}{6}$ of them burned in the oven. How many buns were okay to eat?

   _____

4. A bus has 55 passenger seats. $\frac{2}{5}$ of the seats had passengers. How many seats were empty?

   _____

5. $\frac{2}{3}$ of a number is 18. What is the number?
   ☐ 12   ☐ 18
   ☐ 27   ☐ none of these

6. $\frac{3}{4}$ of a number is 12. What is the number?
   ☐ 4   ☐ 3
   ☐ 9   ☐ none of these

7. What fraction of 20 is 2?
   ☐ $\frac{1}{10}$ ☐ $\frac{1}{2}$
   ☐ $\frac{1}{20}$ ☐ none of these

8. Sinéad has walked 3km of her 24km walk. What fraction of the walk has she done?

   _____

9. How many glasses of juice will the machine hold when it is full? It is now $\frac{5}{6}$ full with 30 glasses of orange juice.

   _____

10. Mr Frosty sells ice-cream cones. On Sunday he sold 24 ninety-nines. This was $\frac{3}{8}$ of all the cones he sold on Sunday. How many cones did he sell that day?

    _____

Topic 16: Chance

A. Warm up!

There's a story that in 1914 a boy tied his bicycle to a tree before going to war. Over many years the tree grew around the bicycle. Do you think this story is likely or unlikely? Why?

_____
_____
_____

B. In your mathematical opinion

1. How many of your favourite sweets are likely to be in a packet? _____
2. Think of something you will probably not do tomorrow. _____
3. Think of something you have never done and probably never will do. _____

C. Experiment

Carry out this experiment 30 times and record your results.
Cut five pieces of card exactly the same size. On one card draw a picture of a light bulb turned on. On each of the other cards draw a picture of a light bulb turned off. Turn the cards upside down and jumble them. Choose a card at random. Record your result. Repeat.

Pair work

	1st	2nd	3rd	4th	5th	6th	7th	8th	9th	10th
	11th	**12th**	**13th**	**14th**	**15th**	**16th**	**17th**	**18th**	**19th**	**20th**
	21st	**22nd**	**23rd**	**24th**	**25th**	**26th**	**27th**	**28th**	**29th**	**30th**

Compare your results with those of your partner.
If the experiment was carried out 100 times altogether, how many times do you think you would choose the light bulb that is turned on? _____

D. Fill the blanks

Fill in the blanks in each sentence.

1. Next month I am likely to _____.
2. It is unlikely that I will _____ on Friday.
3. _____ has no chance of happening.
4. It is almost certain that _____.
5. I will definitely _____.

E. Problems

1. A darts player was blindfolded and threw a dart 20 times at the dartboard you see in the picture. She hit the board every time.
   A tally was kept of the colours she hit.
   What were the likely results?

   red: _____ times
   yellow: _____ times
   blue: _____ times

2. A bag contains cards with the numbers 1 to 10. One card is pulled at random from the bag. Colour the chance sliders to show how likely you think it is that the card chosen is:

   (a) greater than 2
   (This one has been done)
   (b) greater than 0
   (c) greater than 10
   (d) less than 7
   (e) 7
   (f) greater than 9
   (g) odd

Test yourself!

In questions 1 and 2, tick the word that suits best.

1. The world is round.
   - ☐ likely
   - ☐ unlikely
   - ☐ never
   - ☐ definitely

2. Someone chooses a number between 1 and 10. The number is greater than 2.
   - ☐ likely
   - ☐ unlikely
   - ☐ never
   - ☐ definitely

3. A coin is tossed 20 times. How many times are heads likely to appear?
   _____

4. The needle below is most likely to land on which colour?
   _____

5. The needle above is equally likely to land on which two colours?
   _____

6. If I choose a number at random from this list, is the number more likely to be even or odd?

   83, 71, 80, 27, 36, 56, 42, 38, 61

   - ☐ odd
   - ☐ even

7. Write a sentence that includes the word 'unlikely.'
   _____
   _____
   _____

A dice is rolled three times and the numbers rolled are added.

8. What is the greatest possible total?
   _____

9. What is the smallest possible total?
   _____

10. Someone chooses a letter of the alphabet at random. Is the letter more likely to be a vowel or a consonant?
    _____

17 Division 2

A. Warm up!

1. (a) 32 ÷ 4 = _____
   (b) 28 ÷ 7 = _____
   (c) 18 ÷ 2 = _____
   (d) 8 ÷ 1 = _____
   (e) 24 ÷ 8 = _____
   (f) 81 ÷ 9 = _____
   (g) 21 ÷ 3 = _____
   (h) 40 ÷ 5 = _____

2. (a) 24 ÷ 2 = _____
   (b) 72 ÷ 9 = _____
   (c) 36 ÷ 3 = _____
   (d) 56 ÷ 8 = _____
   (e) 28 ÷ 4 = _____
   (f) 42 ÷ 7 = _____
   (g) 60 ÷ 5 = _____
   (h) 48 ÷ 6 = _____

3. (a) 11 ÷ 1 = _____
   (b) 24 ÷ 6 = _____
   (c) 27 ÷ 3 = _____
   (d) 121 ÷ 11 = _____
   (e) 132 ÷ 12 = _____
   (f) 88 ÷ 11 = _____
   (g) 70 ÷ 10 = _____
   (h) 96 ÷ 12 = _____

B. In your mathematical opinion

The answers to each question on the board are wrong. Can you find the correct answer? What mistake did each person make?

Andy = _____
Emma = _____
John = _____
Evan = _____

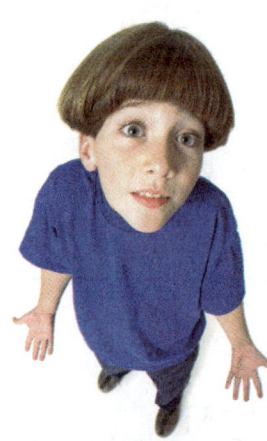

Andy: 4)468 = 112
Emma: 7)742 = 16
John: 6)839 = 139
Evan: 2)617 = 38R1

C. Try these

1. 3)132
2. 5)780
3. 7)931
4. 9)441
5. 12)984
6. 11)561
7. 12)876
8. 10)930

D. Operations

There is no need to work out the answers to these questions. Simply decide if it is an addition, subtraction, multiplication or division question.

1. How many millilitres of milk are left in a bottle if I drink 250 ml? _____

2. A sum of money is shared equally among 12 people. How much did each person get? _____

3. A bag of coins contains 250 twenty cent coins. How many coins are in 5 such bags? _____

4. How many sums have Ava and Eva done if Ava has done 20 and Eva has done 5 more than Ava? _____

E. Real-life maths

Sue's Stationery Shop is having a clearout sale. To sell her old stock, she is putting it into bundles of 2, 3, 4, 5 or 6 and selling the bundles at knockdown prices.

pencil cases:	copies:	rulers:	pens:	pencils:
bundles of 2	bundles of 3	bundles of 4	bundles of 5	bundles of 6
172 in stock	258 in stock	816 in stock	385 in stock	460 in stock

1. How many bundles of pencil cases can be made up? _____

2. How many bundles of each other item can be made up?

   (a) copies: _____

   (b) rulers: _____

   (c) pens: _____

   (d) pencils: _____

3. Sue's pencil cases normally sell at a price of €2·99 each. What price might she charge for a bundle of 2 pencil cases? _____

Test yourself!

In questions 1 and 2 you must get all four sums to answer right to score a point.

1. (a) 24 ÷ 8 = _____
   (b) 27 ÷ 3 = _____
   (c) 77 ÷ 7 = _____
   (d) 54 ÷ 6 = _____

2. (a) 29 ÷ 4 = _____
   (b) 39 ÷ 7 = _____
   (c) 42 ÷ 8 = _____
   (d) 51 ÷ 5 = _____

3. 8) 936
   ☐ 116   ☐ 117
   ☐ 118   ☐ none of these

4. 4) 828
   ☐ 27   ☐ 270
   ☐ 207   ☐ none of these

5. 6) 837
   ☐ 139   ☐ 139 R1
   ☐ 139 R5   ☐ none of these

6. 3) 922
   ☐ 37   ☐ 370 R1
   ☐ 37 R1   ☐ none of these

rough work

7. Sid has sold $\frac{1}{5}$ of his 250 hot dogs. How many hot dogs has he left?
   _____

8. A prize of €250 is shared among Tom and his 3 friends. How much does Tom get if he also gets the remainder?
   _____

9. Divide 250 children among 6 teachers as fairly as possible.
   _____

10. How many of these cartons are needed to safely hold 250 eggs?
    _____

rough work

Topic 18: Decimals 2

A. Warm up!

1 (a) $0.6 + 0.8 =$ _____ (b) $0.02 + 0.07 =$ _____ (c) $0.6 + 6 =$ _____

2 (a) $0.3 + 0.7 =$ _____ (b) $0.04 + 0.07 =$ _____ (c) $0.03 + 5 =$ _____

3 (a) $0.4 + 0.9 =$ _____ (b) $0.05 + 0.05 =$ _____ (c) $0.08 + 0.2 =$ _____

4 (a) $0.9 + 0.9 =$ _____ (b) $0.05 + 0.06 =$ _____ (c) $7 + 0.77 =$ _____

B. Try these

1. (a) 2·15 (b) 3·49 (c) 5·08 (d) 6·20
       4·08   2·08   3·00   0·08
     + 1·87   + 2·77   + 2·72   + 2·99

2. (a) $2 + 0.2 =$
   ☐ 0·4
   ☐ 2·2
   ☐ 0·22
   ☐ none of these

   (b) $0.37 + 7 =$
   ☐ 1·07
   ☐ 0·44
   ☐ 7·37
   ☐ none of these

   (c) $0.08 + 8 =$
   ☐ 8·08
   ☐ 0·88
   ☐ 0·16
   ☐ none of these

   (d) $1.11 + 1 =$
   ☐ 1·12
   ☐ 1·21
   ☐ 2·11
   ☐ none of these

3. (a) $3 - 0.3 =$
   ☐ 3·3
   ☐ 2·7
   ☐ 2·97
   ☐ none of these

   (b) $7 - 0.7 =$
   ☐ 6·93
   ☐ 7·7
   ☐ 6·3
   ☐ none of these

   (c) $8 - 0.4 =$
   ☐ 7·6
   ☐ 4
   ☐ 0·4
   ☐ none of these

   (d) $9 - 0.09 =$
   ☐ 8·1
   ☐ 8·91
   ☐ 0·81
   ☐ none of these

C. Try these

1. 2·16
   x 8

2. 3·79
   x 7

3. 1·59
   x 9

4. 45·6
   x 4

5. 7·09
   x 5

6. 5) 2·35

7. 4) 9·36

8. 3) 8·67

9. 9) 7·56

10. 8) 8·32

D. Problems

1. Share €9 equally among 4 people. _____

2. Chef divided ingredients weighing 2·6kg equally among 4 pots.
   What was the weight of each full pot if an empty pot weighs 0·2kg? _____

E. Real life maths

Each bottle holds one litre when full.

| water | juice | milk | soda | lemonade | cola |
| 0·9l | 0·4l | 0·5l | 0·73l | 0·09l | 0·33l |

1. (a) If I pour the lemonade into the water bottle, will it all fit? _____

   (b) How much space will be left in the water bottle? _____

2. (a) If I pour the cola into the soda bottle, will it fit? _____

   (b) How much cola will be left over? _____

3. How much juice is missing from the juice bottle? _____

4. Which bottle is half full? _____

5. How much liquid is there altogether? _____

Test yourself!

1. Write the following fraction as a decimal.

   $45\frac{9}{100}$ _____

2. Write the following decimal as a fraction: 3·08

   _____

3. Diesel was 102·9c per litre in December. It was 0·15c more in February. What was the price of diesel in February?

   _____

4. Write the following fraction as a decimal: $5\frac{1}{10}$

   ☐ 0·51   ☐ 5·1
   ☐ 5·01   ☐ none of these

5. Find the sum of 3·6 and 0·15

   ☐ 2·1   ☐ 3·45
   ☐ 5·1   ☐ none of these

6. Take 0·05 from 19·33

   ☐ 19·28   ☐ 18·87
   ☐ 14·33   ☐ none of these

rough work

7. Amy was 1·34m in height two years ago. She is now 1·51m. How much has Amy grown?

   _____

8. Marion has 21·78m of string. Raymond has 30·66m more string than Marion. How much string has Raymond?

   _____

9. Three T-shirts cost €7·50. How much for one T-shirt?

   _____

10. Julie earns €8·69 an hour. How much does she earn in an eight hour day?

    _____

rough work

TOPIC 19 Weight

A. In your mathematical opinion

Compare each pair of items. Estimate the weight of the item on the right.

nuts  leaves   snooker balls $2\frac{1}{2}$kg

800g · 380g

jellybeans 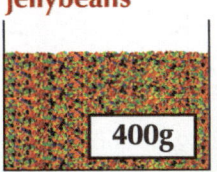  wooden blocks   candy canes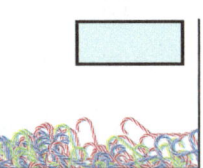

400g · 2·4kg · 420g

B. Calculate!

1. **Change to grams.**
   - (a) 3kg = _____ g
   - (b) 2kg 130g = _____ g
   - (c) 8kg 300g = _____ g
   - (d) 5kg 70g = _____ g
   - (e) 4kg 600g = _____ g
   - (f) $7\frac{1}{2}$ kg = _____ g
   - (g) 1kg 150g = _____ g
   - (h) 3.75kg = _____ g

2. **Write in kilograms using a decimal point.**
   - (a) 4kg 860g = _____ kg
   - (b) 3kg 200g = _____ kg
   - (c) 2kg 120g = _____ kg
   - (d) 7kg 80g = _____ kg
   - (e) 1kg 580g = _____ kg
   - (f) 4,150g = _____ kg
   - (g) 8kg 600g = _____ kg
   - (h) 2,380g = _____ kg

3. **Choose the most likely weight for each item.**

   (a) a school bag with books
   - ☐ 3g
   - ☐ 30g
   - ☐ 300g
   - ☐ 3kg

   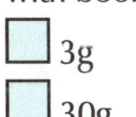

   (b) a pineapple
   - ☐ 10g
   - ☐ 100g
   - ☐ 1kg
   - ☐ 10kg

   (c) a man
   - ☐ 800g
   - ☐ 8kg
   - ☐ 80kg
   - ☐ 800kg

   (d) a watch
   - ☐ 8g
   - ☐ 80g
   - ☐ 800g
   - ☐ 8kg

C. What units?

1. **What units would you use to measure the following? Choose from g, kg, ml, l, cm, m.**
   - (a) length of your finger _____
   - (b) water in a bottle _____
   - (c) weight of a mouse _____
   - (d) weight of a bar of gold _____
   - (e) water in a tank _____
   - (f) length of a garden _____

2. **What is the difference between net weight and gross weight?**
   _____

3. **Write in kilograms and grams.**
   - (a) 4,800g = ___ kg ___ g
   - (b) 2,400g = ___ kg ___ g
   - (c) 3,100g = ___ kg ___ g
   - (d) 3,049g = ___ kg ___ g
   - (e) 6,008g = ___ kg ___ g
   - (f) $4\frac{3}{4}$kg = ___ kg ___ g
   - (g) 2·34kg = ___ kg ___ g
   - (h) 0·04kg = ___ kg ___ g

D. Problems

1. What is the weight of **5** mobile phones if **one** weighs **0·16kg**? _____
2. What is the weight of **1 box** of biscuits if **6 boxes** weigh **3kg 480g**? _____
3. What is the weight of a puppy weighing **4·85kg** less than her Mum who weighs **7kg**? _____

4. What is the weight of **two** pumpkins: one pumpkin weighs **0·95kg** and the other pumpkin weighs **100g** more than the first? _____
5. A jar of jam weighs **454g**. What is the weight of the jam if the jar weighs **46g**? _____

E. Poser

1. Derval has 3 coins. Two of them are the same weight. The third one is a little heavier. How can she find the heavier coin using a balance scales only once?
   _____

2. Cynthia has 3 coins. Two of them are the same weight. The third one is a different weight – it may be heavier or lighter. Can she find the different coin using a balance scales only once? _____

Test yourself!

In questions 1, 2 and 3 choose the most likely weight of each item.

1. One banana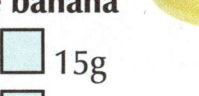
   - ☐ 15g
   - ☐ 150g
   - ☐ 750g
   - ☐ 1kg

2. One sock
   - ☐ 40g
   - ☐ 400g
   - ☐ 800g
   - ☐ 1kg

3. One concrete block
   - ☐ 16kg
   - ☐ 60kg
   - ☐ 600kg
   - ☐ 16kg

4.
   ```
       kg   g
        8  206
   –    2  159
   ```

5.
   ```
       kg   g
        5  180
   ×           7
   ```

6. 8kg 816g ÷ 8 = _____

7. A horse is carrying a jockey weighing 51kg 980g and a saddle weighing 10kg. What weight is the horse carrying?

   _____

8. What weight must I add to a sack weighing 8.43kg to make it weigh 10kg?

   _____

9. What is the weight of 9 packets if one packet weighs 2kg 210g?

   _____

10. What is the weight of one packet if 9 packets weigh 9kg 261g?

    _____

TOPIC 20: 2D Shapes

A. Warm up!

Fun with shapes

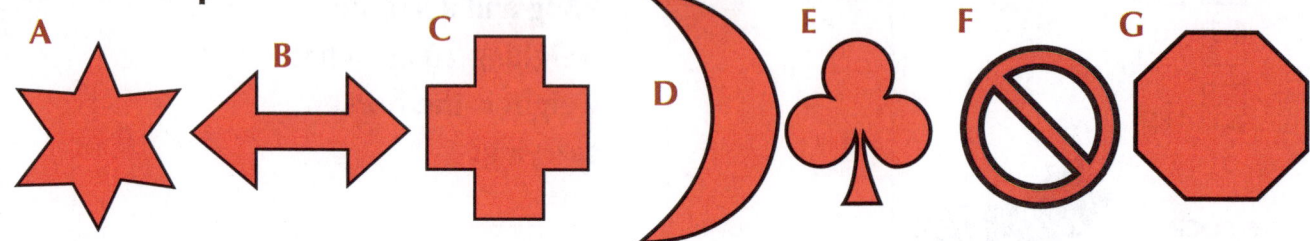

1. Can you name any of the shapes above? _____
   _____

2. Which shape or symbol above might you see in a deck of cards? _____

3. How many sides and how many angles has shape **A**? _____

4. Does shape **B** have symmetry? _____

5. How many of the shapes have symmetry? _____

6. Where might you see shape **D**? _____

7. Shape **C** is used on flags. Which flags? (There are at least 2 correct answers to this!)
   _____

8. If you saw shape **F** as a sign on a door or as a street sign, what might it mean?
   _____

9. How many sides and how many angles has shape **G**? _____

10. Which of the shapes has no straight lines? _____

11. Which of the shapes have right angles? _____

12. Which shapes have obtuse angles? _____

13. Draw your favourite 2D shape. (It does not have to be already drawn on this page.)

B. Try this

1. Find the shape and colour it the same colour as the colour in the text:

   triangle   square   pentagon   hexagon   parallelogram
   octagon   semicircle   rhombus   oval   trapezium

2. One of the shapes may be new to you. It has one pair of parallel lines.
   What is its name? _____

C. Octagon designs

Emily was experimenting with regular octagons to see if they would tessellate.

1. Do octagons tessellate? _____
2. If you used octagonal tiles, what other shape would you use for filling gaps? _____
3. Use the octagons below to colour some original patterns. The first one is done for you.

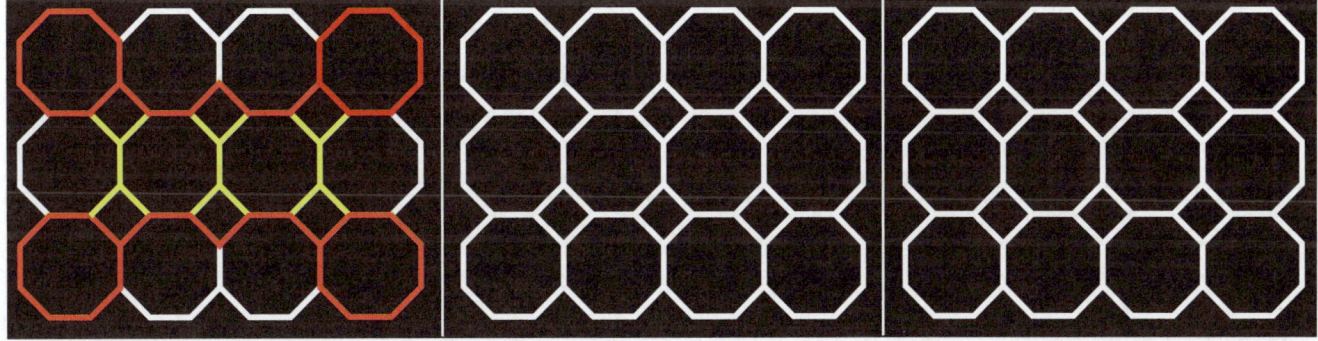

Test yourself!

1. How many more sides has an octagon than a pentagon?

    _____

2. What is the name of this shape? It has 4 sides. Its opposite sides are parallel. Sometimes, but not always, it has 4 right angles. Sometimes, but not always, its touching sides are the same length.

    _____

3. How many diagonals can be drawn in a triangle?
    - ☐ 0
    - ☐ 1
    - ☐ 2
    - ☐ 3

4. What name is given to a rhombus with four right angles?
    - ☐ parallelogram
    - ☐ triangle
    - ☐ trapezium
    - ☐ none of these

5. The answer to a question is *square*. Write a suitable question.

    _____

    _____

rough work

6. Draw a hexagon that is not a regular hexagon.

7. What is the difference between an oval and a circle?

    _____

    _____

8. Draw any shape that has at least one obtuse angle.

9. What name is given to a half circle?

    _____

10. Draw and label different types of triangle.

rough work

TOPIC 21 Patterns

A. Warm up!

Write the next 3 terms of each sequence.

1. 24, 27, 30, 33   ___, ___, ___
2. 32, 40, 48, 56   ___, ___, ___
3. 85, 80, 75, 70   ___, ___, ___
4. 43, 54, 65, 76   ___, ___, ___

B. In your mathematical opinion

1. Each of these sequences has a mistake. Circle it.

   (a) 2, 4, 6, 8, 11, 12, 14
   (b) 4, 8, 12, 15, 20, 24, 28
   (c) 7, 14, 21, 28, 35, 43, 49
   (d) 8, 18, 27, 36, 45, 54, 63
   (e) 44, 55, 66, 77, 88, 99, 111
   (f) 25, 50, 75, 100, 150, 175, 200

2. Complete the missing patterns on the rolls of wallpaper.

3. Draw your own patterns on these rolls.

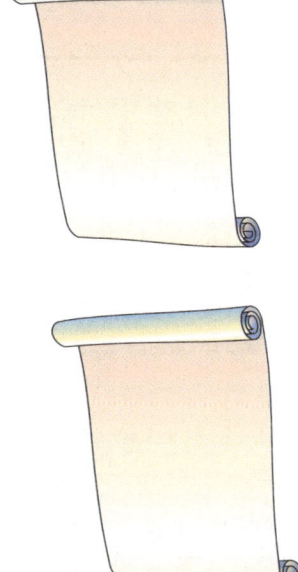

C. Try these

1. What usually comes **immediately before** the following?

   (a) summer _____   (b) morning _____
   (c) October _____   (d) 3·00pm _____
   (e) Friday _____   (f) M _____
   (g) 1,000 _____   (h) IX _____

2. Think of a word that goes **before** each of the following words.

   (**e.g.** tree – oak / Christmas / beech / fir)

   (a) cream _____   (b) key _____
   (c) up _____   (d) door _____
   (e) page _____   (f) bird _____

D. Real life maths

Can you figure out where the third bounce of the ball will happen? (The first two are done.)

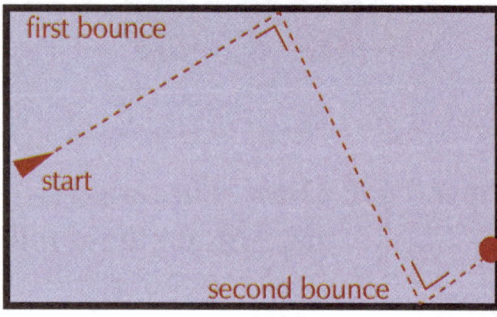
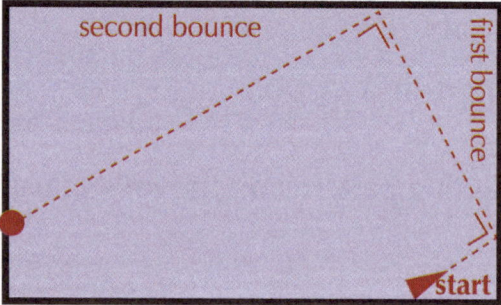

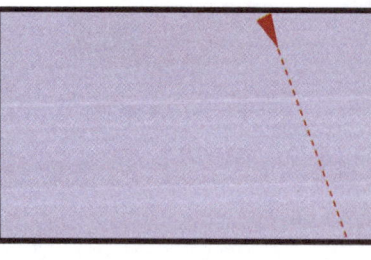
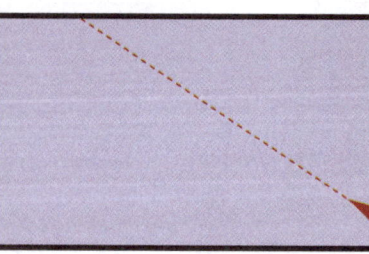

Test yourself!

1. **What comes next?**
   32, 36, 40, 44, 48
   - ☐ 50
   - ☐ 52
   - ☐ 28
   - ☐ none of these

2. **What comes next?**
   99, 93, 87, 81, 75
   - ☐ 70
   - ☐ 74
   - ☐ 59
   - ☐ none of these

3. **What comes next?**
   A, BB, CCC, DDDD, EEEEE
   - ☐ EEEEEE
   - ☐ FFFFF
   - ☐ FFFFFF
   - ☐ none of these

4. **What comes next?**
   $1^1, 2^3, 3^5, 4^7, 5^9$
   - ☐ 6^{10}
   - ☐ 6^{11}
   - ☐ 6^7
   - ☐ none of these

rough work

5. The next number in a sequence is 30. Make up a suitable sequence with at least 4 numbers.

   _____

1	2	3	4	5	6	7	8	9	10
11	12	13	14	15	16	17	18	19	20
21	22	23	24	25	26	27	28	29	30
31	32	33	34	35	36	37	38	39	40
41	42	43	44	45	46	47	48	49	50
51	52	53	54	55	56	57	58	59	60
61	62	63	64	65	66	67	68	69	70
71	72	73	74	75	76	77	78	79	80
81	82	83	84	85	86	87	88	89	90
91	92	93	94	95	96	97	98	99	100

6. Colour the even numbers between 21 and 29 blue.

7. Colour the odd numbers between 80 and 90 red.

8. Colour the multiples of 10 green.

9. Colour the multiples of 3 between 40 and 50 purple.

10. Colour the number that is >30 and <40 and which is a multiple of 9, yellow.

TOPIC 22 Length and Perimeter

A. Warm up!

The sides of each shape are the same length. What is the perimeter of each one?

1. 32m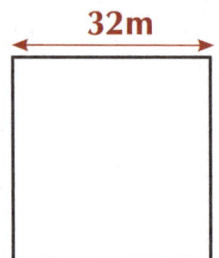
2. 26m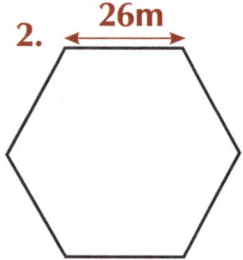
3. 23m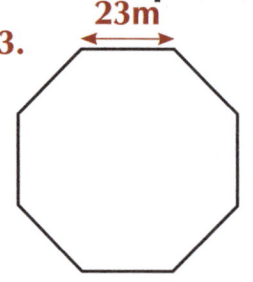
4. 21m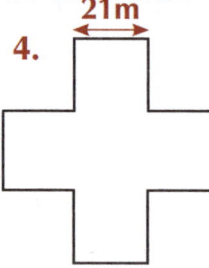

5. 24m
6. 33m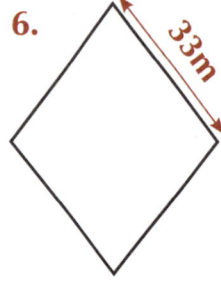
7. 35m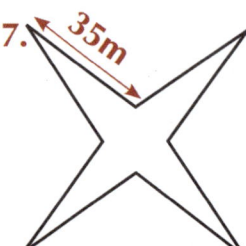
8. 25m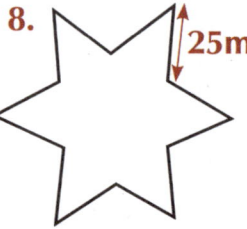

B. Try these

1. Work out the perimeter of the following squares.

    (a) length 8cm _____   (b) length 23cm _____
    (c) length 11cm _____   (d) length 38cm _____
    (e) length 14cm _____   (f) length 86cm _____
    (g) length 19cm _____   (h) length 114cm _____

2. Work out the perimeter of the following rectangles.

    (a) length 10cm width 7cm _____   (e) length 80cm width 22cm _____
    (b) length 12cm width 8cm _____   (f) length 125cm width 42cm _____
    (c) length 15cm width 10cm _____   (g) length 150cm width 80cm _____
    (d) length 20cm width 9cm _____   (h) length 248cm width 52cm _____

3. The width of a rectangle is 65m. Its length is twice its width.

    What is the perimeter of the rectangle? _____

C. True or false?

1. To find the perimeter of a rectangle, you double the length of the rectangle. _____
2. The length of a square is one quarter of its perimeter. _____
3. A perimeter wall would be built around the edge of a property. _____
4. If you are painting a room, you need to know its perimeter. _____
5. If you were building a fence around a garden, you would need to know the perimeter of the garden. _____

D. Real-life maths

A square garden was 12m long. The owner planted trees around the perimeter. The trees were 2m apart. How many trees did he plant?

(**Tip**: Draw a square. Draw a tree in each corner and work from there.)

E. Problems

1. The sides of an equilateral triangle each measure 256m. What is its perimeter? _____
2. A square has sides each 8·5m long. What is its perimeter? _____
3. What is the perimeter of a regular pentagon if each side measures 6·3m? _____
4. A hexagon has sides each measuring 8·4m. What is the perimeter of the hexagon? _____
5. What length is each side of a rhombus if its perimeter is 120m? _____
6. What length is each side of an equilateral triangle if its perimeter measures 186m? _____
7. What length is each side of an octagon if each its perimeter is 60m long? _____

F. Poser

The following question has two correct answers. Can you find both?

The perimeter of an isosceles triangle measures 40cm. One of the sides is 16cm long.

What are the lengths of the other two sides? **(a)** _____ **(b)** _____

Test yourself!

1.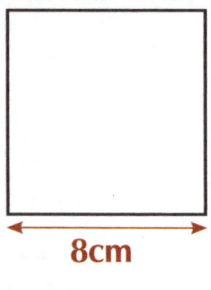
   8cm

   perimeter: _____

2.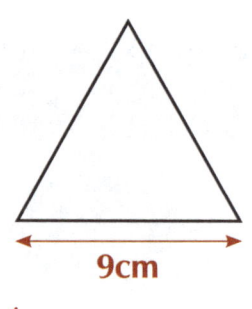
   9cm

   perimeter: _____

3.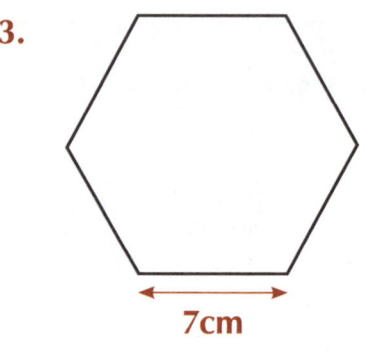
   7cm

   perimeter: _____

4. A rectangle is 20cm long and 4cm wide. What is its perimeter?
   ☐ 80cm ☐ 24cm
   ☐ 48cm ☐ none of these

5. The perimeter of a square measures 36cm. How long is each side of the square?
   ☐ 6cm   ☐ 9cm
   ☐ 144cm ☐ none of these

6. The perimeter of a rectangle is 100cm. The length of the rectangle is 30cm. What is the width of the rectangle?
   ☐ 130cm ☐ 260cm
   ☐ 20cm ☐ none of these

7. If you walked <u>twice</u> around a square field whose sides each measure 40m, how far would you walk?
   _____

8. An isosceles triangle has a perimeter of 100cm. Two of the sides each measure 40cm. What is the length of the third side? _____

9. Write a perimeter question the answer to which is 80m.
   _____

10. The answer to a multiple choice perimeter question is 48m. Write a suitable question and give 3 wrong answers as well as the right answer.
    _____
    _____

70 Planet Maths Activity Book • 4th Class

TOPIC 23 Area

A. Warm up!

Choose the one that is likely to have the greater area. There are two trick questions!

1. Cork or Wicklow
2. Earth's land or Earth's oceans
3. Cinema screen or TV screen
4. Limerick to Waterford or Limerick to Belfast
5. Lough Neagh or Lough Corrib
6. mat or carpet
7. Mobile phone screen or computer screen
8. square or rectangle

B. In your mathematical opinion

What is the approximate area of each shadow picture?

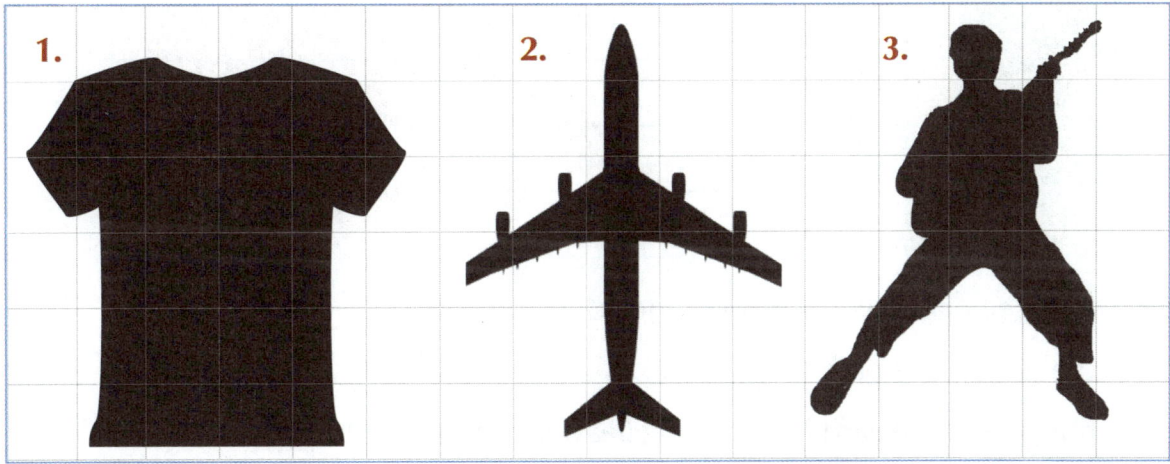

1.
2.
3.

C. Calculate!

1. A pond in a garden has an area of 22m². If the area of the whole garden is 131m², what is the area of the garden excluding (leaving out) the pond? _____

2. The area of a roof is 82m². The roof has 2 solar panels, each with an area of 7m². What is the area of the part of the roof excluding the solar panels? _____

D. Real-life maths

Rose has planted a variety of flowers in her flower beds. The area of each square is 1m².

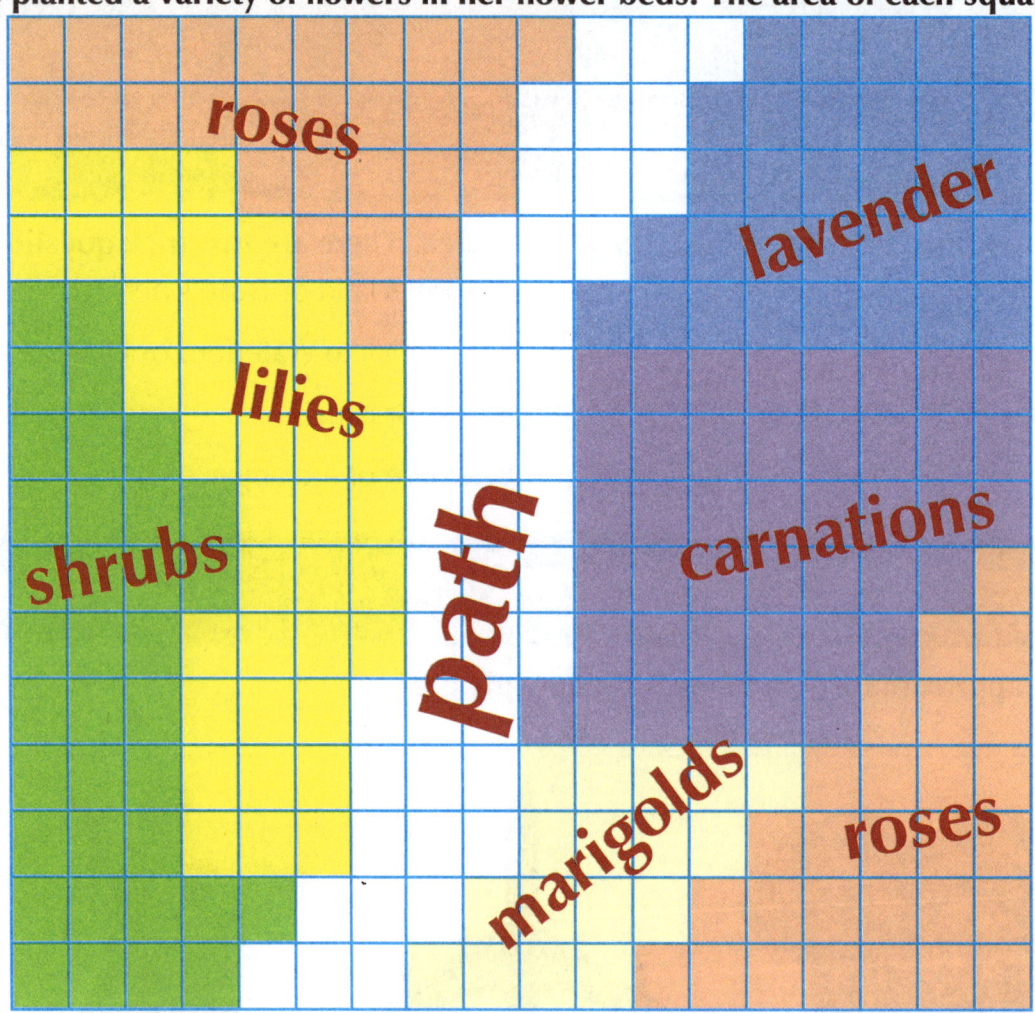

1. What is the area of the whole garden, including the path? _____
2. What is the area of the path? _____
3. What is the area of the garden excluding (*leaving out*) the path? _____
4. Write how many square metres Rose has planted of the following.

    (a) shrubs _____   (b) marigolds _____   (c) roses _____

    (d) carnations _____   (e) lavender _____   (f) lilies _____

5. Which flower do you think is Rose's favourite? _____
6. How many marigolds are in Rose's garden if 15 marigolds grow in each square metre? _____
7. Rose sells her carnations to the local florist. She gets €1 for a bunch of 5 carnations.

    (a) How much will Rose earn for 400 carnations? _____

    (b) How much will the florist earn if he sells all the carnations at €3 per bunch? _____

Test yourself!

1. Number these in order of area. Start with the smallest.
   - ☐ field
   - ☐ page
   - ☐ floor
   - ☐ tabletop

2. A field has an area of 2,000m². There are some trees planted in the field covering an area of 485m². What is the area of the part of the field around the trees?

   _____   Trees 485m²

3. Name something with an approximate area of 1m².

   _____

4. [6m]
   The area of the coloured part is:
   - ☐ 24m
   - ☐ 24m²
   - ☐ 20m
   - ☐ none of these

5. [6m]
   The area of the coloured part is:
   - ☐ 28m
   - ☐ 25m²
   - ☐ 20m²
   - ☐ none of these

6. The answer to a question is 32m². Write a suitable question.

   _____
   _____

7. Draw a square with an area of 25cm².

8. Draw a rectangle with an area of 18cm².

9. An apartment block has 4 floors with a total area of 504m². What is the area of one floor?

   _____

10. A greenhouse has 90 panes of glass. The area of one pane is half of a square metre. What is the area of glass in the greenhouse? _____

TOPIC 24 Time 2

A. Warm up!

Fill the missing terms in these time trail patterns.

1.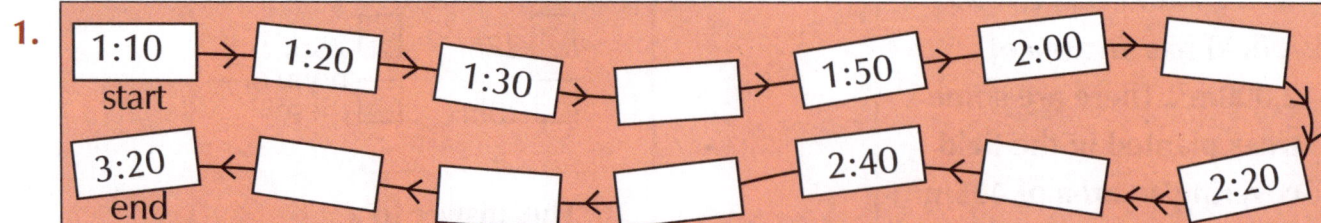

2.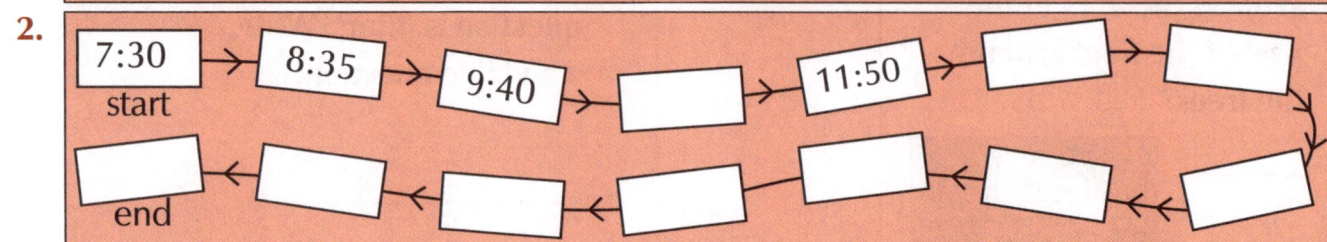

3.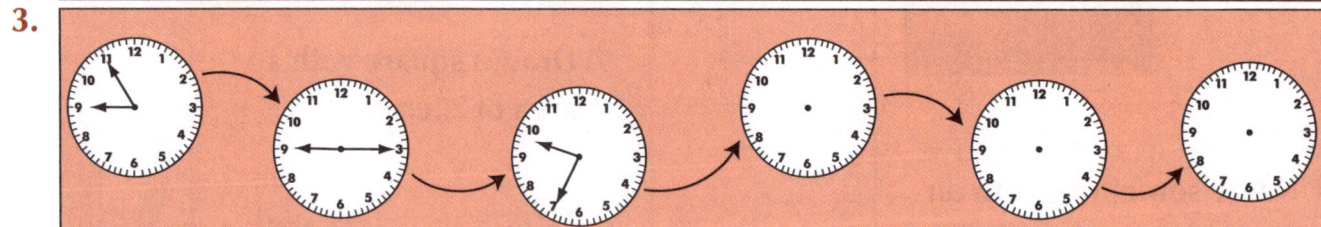

4.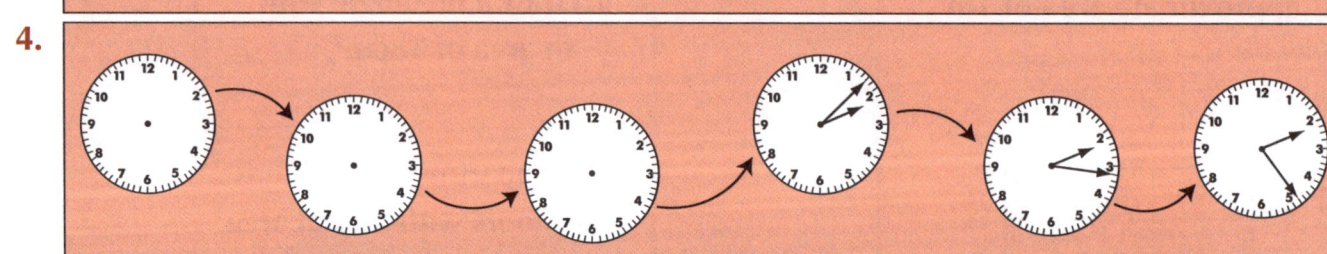

B. Try these

1. Change the hours and minutes to minutes.

   (a) 1 hour 15 mins _____

   (b) 1 hour 30 mins _____

   (c) 1 hour 55 mins _____

   (d) 2 hours 5 mins _____

   (e) 2 hours 20 mins _____

2. Change the minutes to hours and minutes.

   (a) 70 minutes _____

   (b) 75 minutes _____

   (c) 85 minutes _____

   (d) 91 minutes _____

   (e) 103 minutes _____

C. Estimate

Think of something that might take:

1. 5 seconds _____
2. 5 minutes _____
3. 5 hours _____
4. 5 weeks _____
5. 5 years _____
6. 5 months _____

D. Real-life maths

1. Each clock is 15 minutes slow. Show the correct time beneath each digital clock:

2. Look at the dentist's appointment book.

Time	Client	Treatment
9:20 am	Ms Pearly Whites	check-up
9:40 am	Ms V.M. Pyre	infusion
10:15 am	Mr K. Nine	tracks
11:00 am	Coffee Break	
11:30 am	Mr F. Loss	cleaning
12:15 pm	Lunch Break	
1:30 pm	Ms H. Crown	whitening
2:10 pm	Ms E. N. Amel	check-up
2:30 pm	Mr Den Ture	false teeth fitting
3:50 pm	Mr M. Olar	extraction
4:30 pm	Mr Sor Ghums	cavity

(a) Which client has an appointment at 10:15 am? _____

(b) How long does the dentist expect to be with Ms Crown? _____

(c) Whose appointment ends at 4:30 pm? _____

(d) How long does a check-up take? _____

(e) How much time does the dentist take for lunch? _____

(f) If the dentist got an emergency call from a client, at what time might the client be fitted in? _____

(g) At what time do you expect the dentist will finish? _____

(h) With which client will the dentist spend the greatest length of time? _____

Test yourself!

1. Change to hours and minutes.

(a) 93 minutes

_____

(b) 125 minutes

_____

2. Change to minutes.

(a) 1 hour 25 minutes

_____

(b) $2\frac{1}{4}$ hours

_____

3. What time comes 25 minutes after 2:45pm?

_____

4. How many times does the long hand go around the clock face in 24 hours?

_____

5. hrs   mins
         3   38
         1   44
      + 2   53
      ─────────────
   ☐ 7 hrs 35 mins
   ☐ 8 hrs 15 mins
   ☐ 7 hrs 15 mins
   ☐ none of these

6. hrs   mins
         6   38
      − 1   54
      ─────────────
   ☐ 5 hrs 24 mins
   ☐ 4 hrs 84 mins
   ☐ 4 hrs 44 mins
   ☐ none of these

7. A movie double bill begins at 5:55pm and ends at 8:40pm. For how long does the second movie last if the first movie lasts for 1 hour 20 minutes? _____

8. At what time should I leave for a 3:15pm appointment if the journey will take 1 hour 20 minutes? _____

9. A bus leaves at 8:25am and arrives at 12:10pm. For how long was it travelling if it stopped for a 15-minute break?

_____

10. How many times does the short hand go around the clock face in 24 hours? _____

TOPIC 25 Operations

A. Warm up!

Tot' em Up	Tot' em Up	Tot' em Up	Tot' em Up	Tot' em Up	Tot' em Up	Tot' em Up	Tot' em Up	Tot' em Up	Tot' em Up
2	3	4	2	5	3	2	1	8	7
8	6	8	5	5	5	9	7	5	5
5	9	1	7	6	3	5	9	7	3
5	1	8	4	6	9	3	7	2	3
8	4	3	6	8	3	8	5	2	1
+3	+7	+8	+2	+4	+7	+7	+3	+6	+9

B. In your mathematical opinion

1. **Estimate the answers to these questions. Round to nearest 100.**

   (a) 480 + 610 + 270 = _____   (b) 987 − 271 = _____

   (c) 180 + 680 + 315 = _____   (d) 882 − 314 = _____

2. **Estimate the answers to these questions. Round to nearest 1,000.**

   (a) 4,700 + 1,100 + 3,200 = _____   (b) 8,942 − 3,677 = _____

   (c) 4,400 + 2,800 + 976 = _____   (d) 7,049 − 3,992 = _____

C. Calculate!

1. 4129
   2233
   + 2377

2. 1595
   2323
   + 5677

3. 4284
   3476
   + 258

4. 8358
   − 2166

5. 7429
   − 2773

6. 8742
   − 2358

7. 975
   x 7

8. 886
   x 9

9. 89
   x 60

10. 73
    x 87

11. 129
    x 18

12. 213
    x 24

13. 5)815

14. 6)738

15. 9)576

16. 4)832

17. 8)792

Based on Planet Maths 4 pages 152, 153, 154, 155 and 156

D. Brackets

1. 50 – (8 + 9) = ____
2. 3 x (20 + 40) = ____
3. 50 – (7 x 6) = ____
4. 3 x (100 – 1) = ____
5. 50 – (32 ÷ 4) = ____
6. 3 x (8 x 8) = ____
7. 50 – (50 – 50) = ____
8. 3 x (265 ÷ 5) = ____
9. 30 – 5 + 8 = ____
10. 30 – 23 – 4 = ____
11. 30 – 9 + 7 = ____
12. 30 – 18 – 7 = ____

Start inside the brackets

E. Problems

1. Mr Moneybags has €50 in his wallet and €20 in his pocket. He spent €10 at the fruit market and €15 at the vegetable stall. How much has he left? _____

2. 234 cards were shared equally among 9 boys. Each boy gave half of his share to his sister. How many cards did each girl get? _____

3. A case contains 8 boxes of chocolates. Each box contains 20 chocolates. How many chocolates are in 10 cases? _____

F. Cross number puzzle

Across:
1. 2149 + 2386 = ___
3. 1596 + 7140 = ___
5. 1488 + 3684 = ___
6. 5008 + 2147 = ___
7. 46 + 46 = ___
8. 3687 + 3280 = ___
10. 4837 + 2460 = ___
12. 159 + 752 = ___
13. 2588 + 3090 = ___
14. 6238 + 547 = ___

Down:
1. 9157 – 4406 = ___
2. 5264 – 1394 = ___
3. 9000 – 539 = ___
4. 7058 – 3913 = ___
6. 8500 – 8428 = ___
7. 4308 – 3337 = ___
9. 8126 – 1179 = ___
11. 9999 – 991 = ___

Test yourself!

1. A warehouse stored 4,600 frozen pizzas. Last week 3,850 of these pizzas were delivered to supermarkets. 3,480 new pizzas were delivered to the warehouse. How many pizzas are now in the warehouse?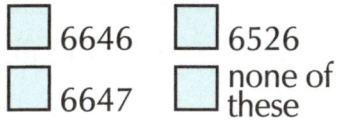

   _____

2. A bus company carried 1,256 passengers on Saturday and 183 more than that on Sunday. How many passengers did it carry altogether during the weekend?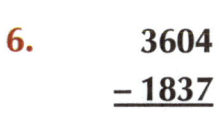

   _____

3. A leaflet company delivers leaflets to houses. On Friday, 9,000 leaflets were shared equally among 4 delivery people. How many leaflets did they each deliver?

   _____

4. How many gigabytes of information can a computer store? It has 4 drives and each drive can hold 780 gigabytes?

   _____

5. 2138
    1449
   + 3059

   ☐ 6646   ☐ 6526
   ☐ 6647   ☐ none of these

6. 3604
   − 1837

   ☐ 2233   ☐ 1777
   ☐ 1767   ☐ none of these

7. 148
   x 27

   ☐ 1332   ☐ 3646
   ☐ 3886   ☐ none of these

8. (72 ÷ 3) x 4 = _____

9. 12 − 5 + 2 = _____

10. The answer to a word problem is 2,560 bags. Write a suitable problem

    _____

    _____

    _____

TOPIC 26 Capacity

A. Warm up!

1. How much liquid is in each container?

(a) 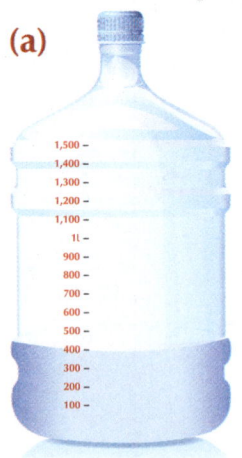 (b) 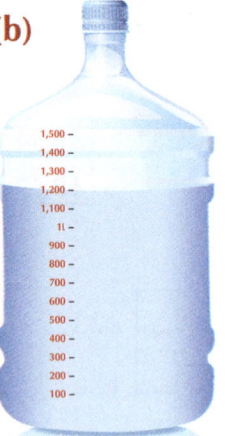 (c) 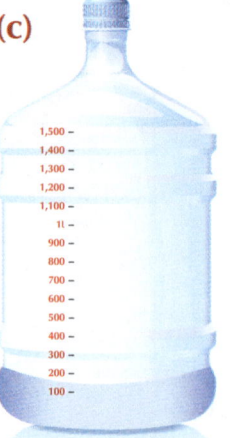 (d)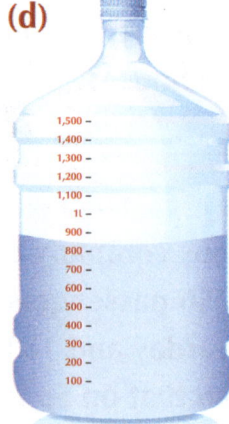

2. Colour these containers to show the correct amounts of liquid.

800ml   1·2l   0·65l $1\frac{1}{4}$l

(a) 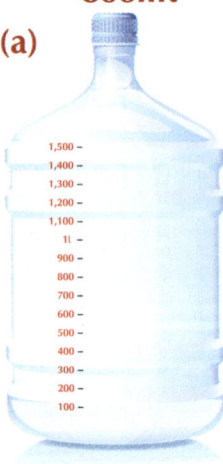 (b) 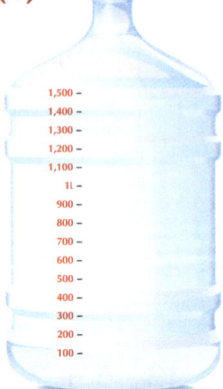 (c) 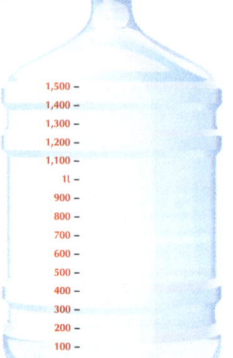 (d)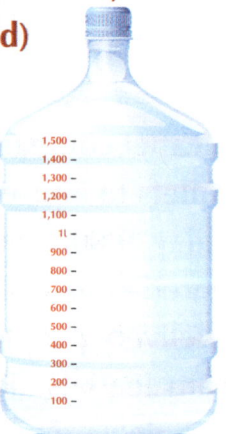

B. Try these

Change to l and ml: Example: 4·23l = 4l 230ml

1. 5·39l = _____
2. 2·9l = _____
3. 4190ml = _____
4. 8·14l = _____
5. 3·8l = _____
6. 6008ml = _____
7. 2·19l = _____
8. 1·08l = _____
9. $2\frac{1}{4}$l = _____
10. 3·41l = _____
11. 2225ml = _____
12. 7310l = _____

C. Try these

1. Write in millilitres. e.g. 4l 230ml = 4230ml
   - (a) 2l 180ml = _____
   - (b) 3l 123ml = _____
   - (c) $8\frac{1}{2}$l = _____
   - (d) 4l 136ml = _____
   - (e) 8l 59ml = _____
   - (j) 6.45ml = _____
   - (c) 9l 800ml = _____
   - (g) 2l 2ml = _____
   - (k) 6.4l = _____
   - (d) 5l 760ml = _____
   - (h) 6l 60ml = _____
   - (l) 6.04l = _____

2. Write in litres using a decimal point. e.g. 3l 420ml = 3·42l
   - (a) 6l 780ml = _____
   - (e) 1l 110ml = _____
   - (i) $3\frac{1}{4}$l = _____
   - (b) 2l 120ml = _____
   - (f) 8l 900ml = _____
   - (j) $5\frac{3}{4}$l = _____
   - (c) 3l 730ml = _____
   - (g) 2l 200ml = _____
   - (k) 6l = _____
   - (d) 8l 570ml = _____
   - (h) 3l 330ml = _____
   - (l) 4l = _____

3. Now try these.

(a) l	(b) l	(c) l	(d) l	(e) l
2·45	1·96	4·08	3·39	5·55
+ 1·38	+ 2·55	+ 2·19	+ 6·38	+ 3·77

4. (a) 8l 560ml – 5l 230ml = _____
   (b) 6l – 60ml = _____
   (c) 9l 80ml – 2l 450ml = _____
   (d) 12l 20ml – 4l 15ml = _____

5. (a) 6 x 2·15l = _____
   (b) 8 x 8·19l = _____
   (c) 4 x 5·69l = _____
   (d) 9 x 7·69l = _____

6. (a) 7·36l ÷ 4 = _____
   (b) 5·4l ÷ 4 = _____
   (c) 8·82l ÷ 9 = _____
   (d) 8l ÷ 5 = _____

E. Problems

1. How many times can I fill a $1\frac{1}{2}$ litre bottle from a tank containing 5 litres? _____
2. How many litres do I have if I have 20 cartons, each with $\frac{1}{4}$ litre? _____
3. A recipe needs 1 litre of a special ingredient that is sold in 150ml sachets. How many sachets will I need to buy? _____

Test yourself!

1. $2.68l + 3\frac{1}{2}l =$ _____

2. $9l - 1.35l =$ _____

3. $7 \times 2.38l =$ _____

4. $3.9l \div 2 =$ _____

5. 4,080ml is the same as
   - ☐ 4l 8ml
   - ☐ 4l 80ml
   - ☐ 4l 800ml
   - ☐ none of these

6. 7·2l is the same as
   - ☐ 7l 2ml
   - ☐ 7l 20ml
   - ☐ 7l 200ml
   - ☐ none of these

7. A watering can is likely to hold approximately
   - ☐ 5ml   ☐ 50ml
   - ☐ 5l   ☐ 50l

rough work

8. How much fuel is left in a 10 litre tank if 3l 350 ml of fuel is used?

   _____

9. Tara poured 3 jugs each with 2l 450ml of water into a bucket. How much water is in the bucket?

   _____

10. One and a half litres of orange juice is shared among 6 children. How much will each child get?

    _____

rough work

TOPIC 27 Problem Solving

A. Word problems

Complete the sentences.

1. (a) Desert is to sand as ocean is to _____.
   (b) Arm is to hand as leg is to _____.
   (c) Leg is to knee as arm is to _____.
   (d) Dog is to bark as duck is to _____.
   (e) Mouse is to small as elephant is to _____.
   (f) School is to pupil as hospital is to _____.
   (g) School is to teacher as hospital is to _____.
   (h) Fish is to swim as snake is to _____.
   (i) Fire is to hot as ice is to _____.
   (j) Itch is to scratch as broken is to _____.

2. (a) 2 is to even as 3 is to _____.
   (b) x is to multiply as ÷ is to _____.
   (c) l is to ml as kg is to _____.
   (d) Hour is to minute as minute is to _____.
   (e) Sum is to add as product is to _____.
   (f) 9 is to 18 as 12 is to _____.
   (g) 14 is to 7 as 36 is to _____.
   (h) Quadrilateral is to 4 as triangle is to _____.
   (i) Pentagon is to 5 is octagon is to _____.
   (j) Cube is to 6 as triangular prism is to _____.

B. Picture problems

Draw the missing symbols.

1.  is to  as  is to

2. is to 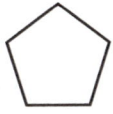 as is to

3.  is to  as  is to

4. ABC is to ƆᗺA as DEF is to

5.  is to  as is to

6. 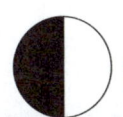 is to  as  is to

C. More problems

1. A fire station gets a call at 10:55am. The fire engine arrives at the emergency in 8 minutes. At what time did the fire engine arrive? _____

2. An aquarium has the following fish in its catalogue:

black neons: 30	angelfish: out of stock	clownfish: 88	catfish: 28
goldfish: 48	black mollies: 12	koi: 2	

   How many fish are available for sale altogether? _____

3. The school secretary booked a bus for the class tour costing €220. The entry fee to the museum is €3 per child and €5 per adult. What is the total cost of the trip if 28 pupils go on the trip and teacher brings one adult to help? _____

4. How much to buy two books online if each book costs €9·99 and there is a postage and packaging charge of €3·49? _____

5. Dad booked flights for a family of 5 (including Dad) costing €89 per flight. What was the total bill if there were extra charges as follows? Airport tax: €10 per person. Government tax: €5 per person. _____

6. Three times a number is 48. What is half of the number? _____

7. A lighthouse flashes 12 times per minute. How many times will it flash in an hour? _____

8. A shop reduced all it prices in a sale by a quarter. What is the sale price of these items?

Jeans €44 _____	Shirts €24 _____	T-Shirts €16 _____	Jumpers €28 _____
Shoes €48 _____	Skirts €32 _____	Hats €22 _____	Socks €5 _____

9. A recipe needs 500g of ground almonds. How many packets should I buy if each packet contains 150g of ground almonds? _____

10. How long will it take an empty garden pond to fill with water if the pond can hold 1,000 litres of water and water is flowing at a rate of 10 litres per minute? _____

11. A rectangular floor is 6m long and 4m wide. What is the area of the floor? _____

12. The weather forecaster predicts that Tuesday's temperature will be 2° warmer than Monday's temperature of 11 °C. The forecaster then said that Wednesday is likely to be 3° colder than Tuesday. What is the temperature likely to be on Wednesday? _____

13. The perimeter of a rectangular corridor is 18m. If the corridor is 7m long, what is its width? _____

14. What is the whole number if $\frac{3}{4}$ of it is 24? _____

Test yourself!

1. Which two letters lie in the middle of the alphabet?

______

2. Celia has €112. Delia has €20 more than that. How much money have they altogether?

______

3. A reel holds 10m of string. How much string is left if I cut off $\frac{1}{2}$m to wrap a parcel and use two 70cm lengths to lace my boots?

______

4. Multiply the difference between 8 and 12 by the sum of 5 and 6.

- ☐ 20
- ☐ 15
- ☐ 44
- ☐ none of these

5. How long did Nathan spend training if he was 1 hour 54 minutes in the gym and was running for 58 minutes?

- ☐ 2 hours 12 minutes
- ☐ 2 hours 52 minutes
- ☐ 1 hour 102 minutes
- ☐ none of these

rough work

6. ● is to ○ as ■ is to

7. KLM is to **MLK** as HIJ is to

8. Make up an analogy like those in question 6 and 7.

______

______

9. The answer to a problem is €12·50. Write a suitable problem.

10. The sheet of paper in the diagram is 5cm wide. Draw a vertical line to divide the page in two so that one side is 1cm wider than the other. (There are two ways to do this).

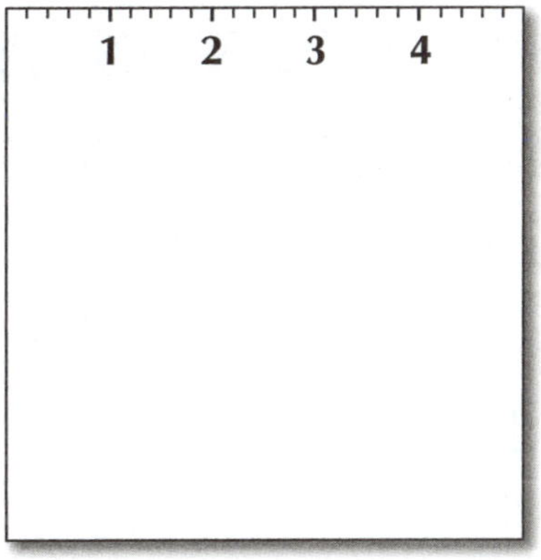

rough work

TOPIC 28 — 3D Shapes

A. Count the cubes

Each of these shapes is made of cubes. How many cubes were used to make each one?

1.  ____
2. 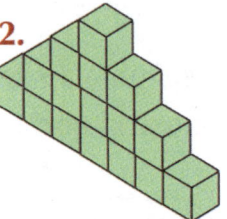 ____
3.  ____
4. 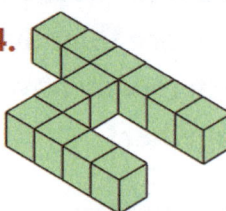 ____
5. 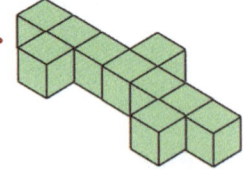 ____
6. 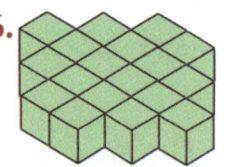 ____
7. 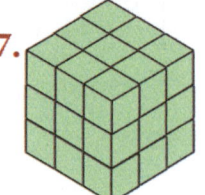 ____
8.  ____
9. 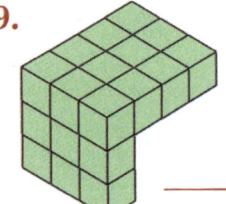 ____
10.  ____
11. 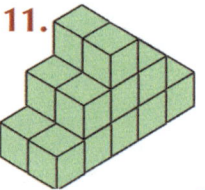 ____
12. 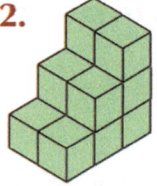 ____
13.  ____
14.  ____
15.  ____
16.  ____

B. Fill in the blanks

1. A _____ has 6 faces, each in the shape of a square.
2. A _____ may be sliced in such a way that all slices are the same size.
3. If I place 5 cubes together in a straight line I will make a _____.
4. Most 3D shapes have more _____ than faces.
5. A pentagonal prism has _____ vertices.
6. A triangular prism has _____ faces.

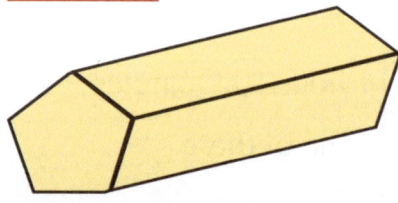

C. Fill in the blanks

1. A _____ is like a pyramid built on a circle.
2. A pentagonal pyramid has _____ faces.
3. The D in 3D stands for _____..
4. The shape with the greatest number of faces that I can think of is the _____.
5. A _____ may be sliced in such a way that each slice is smaller than the one before.

D. Colour the shapes

Colour the 3D shapes using the instructions below.

1. faces of cylinder: red
2. faces of triangular prism: yellow
3. vertices of pyramid: green
4. faces of cuboid: green
5. edges of triangular prism: black
6. edges of cylinder: black
7. edges of cuboid: red
8. faces of hexagonal prism: blue
9. edges of pyramid: red
10. vertices of triangular prism: red
11. vertices of cuboid: blue
12. vertices of hexagonal prism: yellow
13. edges of hexagonal prism: black
14. faces of pyramid: blue

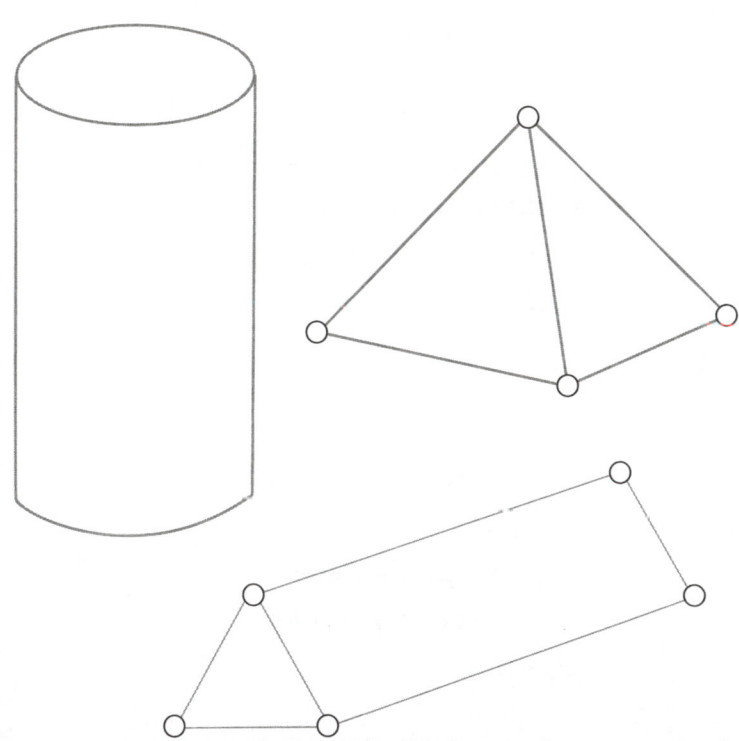
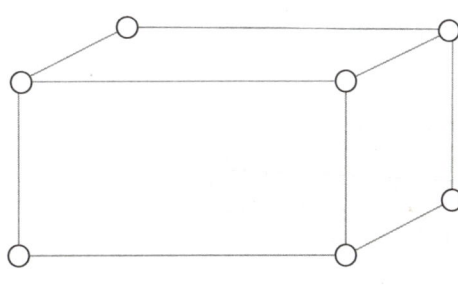
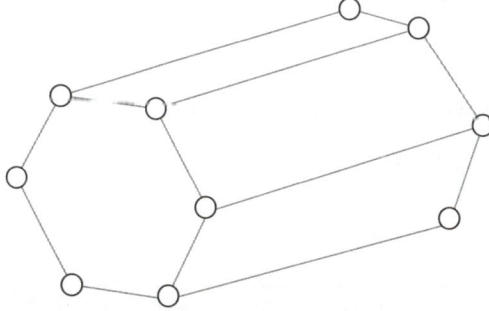

Test yourself!

1. How many faces has a cube? ____

2. How many edges has this square pyramid? ____

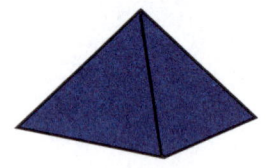

3. How many vertices has this prism? ____

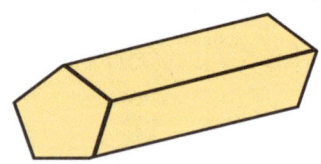

4. Name this shape.

☐ cube ☐ pyramid
☐ cylinder ☐ none of these

5. Name two 3D shapes that will stack easily.

_____
_____

6. If you slice a _____, the slices get smaller and smaller.

7. Name this shape.

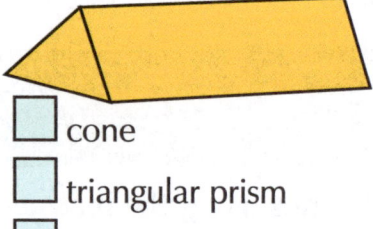

☐ cone
☐ triangular prism
☐ triangular pyramid
☐ none of these

8. Name this shape.

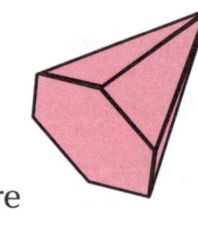

☐ sphere
☐ cone
☐ hexagonal pyramid
☐ none of these

9. What is the difference between a 2D shape and a 3D shape?

_____

10. The answer to a question on a 3D shape is 'pentagonal prism'. Write a suitable question.

Topic 29: Number Sentences

A. Warm up!

Fill the blanks in these addition number sentences.

1. 4 + ☐ = 12
2. 16 + ☐ = 32
3. 35 + ☐ = 90
4. 7 + ☐ = 19
5. 20 + ☐ = 50
6. 42 + ☐ = 100
7. 9 + ☐ = 20
8. 25 + ☐ = 60
9. 4 + 8 + ☐ = 30
10. 10 + ☐ = 25
11. 30 + ☐ = 70
12. 5 + 11 + ☐ = 28
13. 12 + ☐ = 30
14. 32 + ☐ = 64
15. 7 + ☐ + 15 = 22

B. Try these

1. A music collection has 30 tunes on 3 disks. One of the disks has 9 tunes and another disk has 11 tunes. How many tunes are on the third disk? Write a number sentence.

   _____

2. 95 pirates board 3 boats and sail for Treasure Island. One of the boats has 30 pirates. Another boat has the captain and 30 pirates. How many pirates are aboard the third boat? Write a number sentence.

   _____

3. Fill the blanks in these subtraction number sentences.

   (a) 10 − ☐ = 7
   (b) 30 − ☐ = 1
   (c) 50 − ☐ = 14
   (d) 15 − ☐ = 4
   (e) 33 − ☐ = 20
   (f) 52 − ☐ = 26
   (g) 20 − ☐ = 8
   (h) 40 − ☐ = 25
   (i) 60 − ☐ = 14
   (j) 22 − ☐ = 11
   (k) 44 − ☐ = 16
   (l) 100 − ☐ = 24

4. A dealer deals a number of cards from a deck of 52 cards leaving 39 cards in the deck. How many cards did she deal? Write a number sentence.

   _____

5. 16 guests arrive at Sarah's party. 3 of the guests leave early. How many people are left at the party altogether? Write a number sentence.

   _____

C. Real-life maths

Mrs T wishes to park her car for one hour. Parking costs 75c per hour. A parking machine takes coins and does not give change. What coins should Mrs T insert in the parking machine so that she pays at least 75c each time? Circle them.

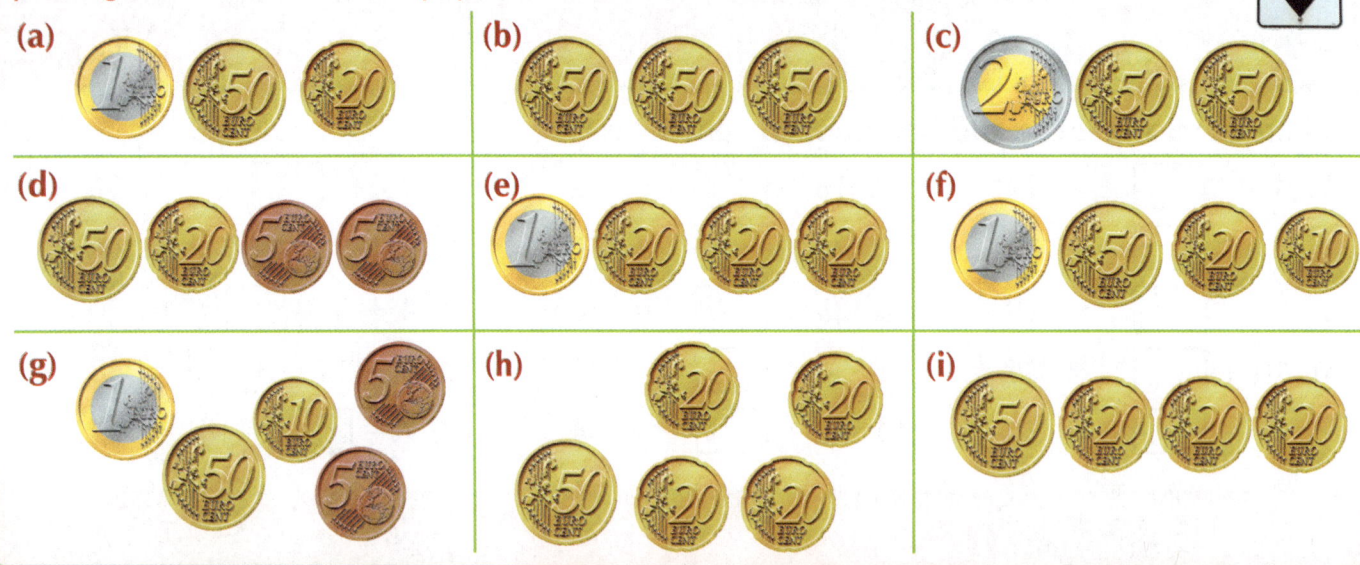

D. Poser

1. Mrs T has 7 coins totalling 50c. What coins are they? _____
2. Mrs T has 12 coins totalling €1. What coins are they? _____
3. Mrs T has 7 coins totalling €5. What coins are they? _____

E. Poser

You are setting out to cross a wide desert and you need to bring as much water as you can. Your camel can carry as many water skins as you wish, so long as the total is no greater than 50 litres. Which water skins should you bring in each box below? Circle them.

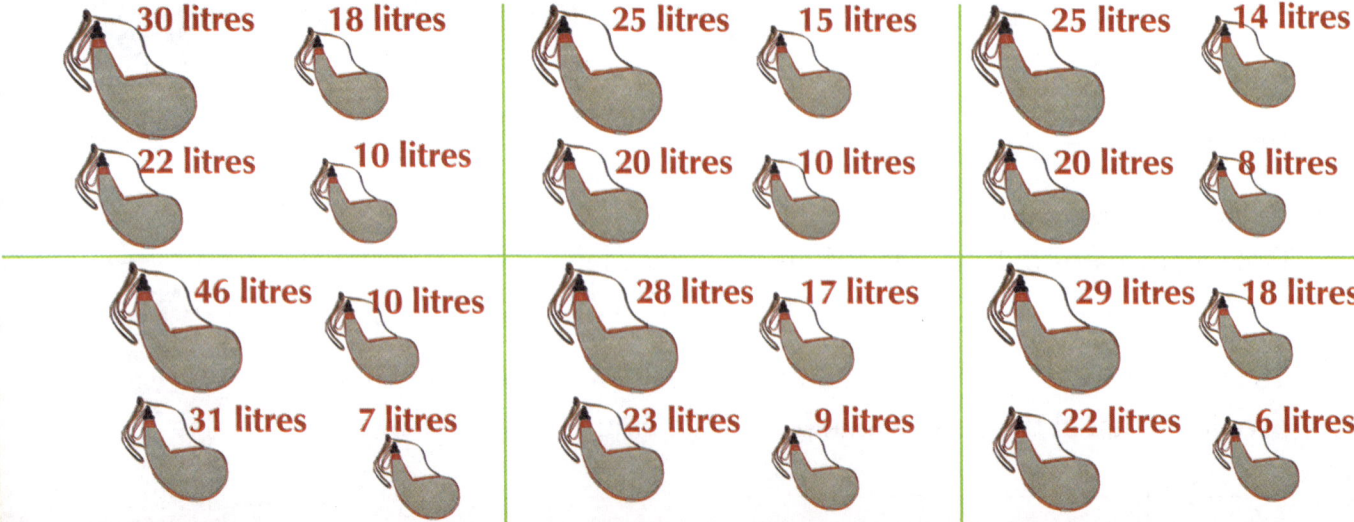

Test yourself!

1. Fill the blanks in this number sentence.

   7 + __ = 14

2. Fill the blanks in this number sentence.

   8 − __ = 3

3. Fill the blanks in this number sentence.

   4 sets of __ = 12

4. Fill the blanks in this number sentence.

   12 ÷ __ = 2

5. What is the greatest whole number I can put in the blank space to make the sentence true:

   50 + __ < 60
   ☐ 1   ☐ 9
   ☐ 10 ☐ none of these

6. What is the smallest whole number I can put in the blank space to make the sentence true:

   50 + __ > 75
   ☐ 25 ☐ 30
   ☐ 24 ☐ none of these

rough work

7. Which two numbers will make this number sentence true:

   8 + __ + __ = 20
   ☐ 6 and 7
   ☐ 1 and 19
   ☐ 10 and 10
   ☐ 4 and 8

8. Write a number sentence and solve the problem. Julie has saved €20. She wishes to buy a computer game costing €50. How much more does Julie need to save?

9. Write a number sentence and solve the problem. There are 18 birds perched in a tree. 7 of the birds flew away. How many birds are left?

10. Write a number sentence and solve the problem. An artist stores her paint brushes in sets of 5. How many sets has she if she has 30 brushes altogether?

rough work

TOPIC 30 Problem Solving 2

A. Warm up!

1. These 3 patterns show traffic lights changing colour. The numbers at the bottom show seconds. Can you colour the lights and the timelines to finish the 3 patterns?

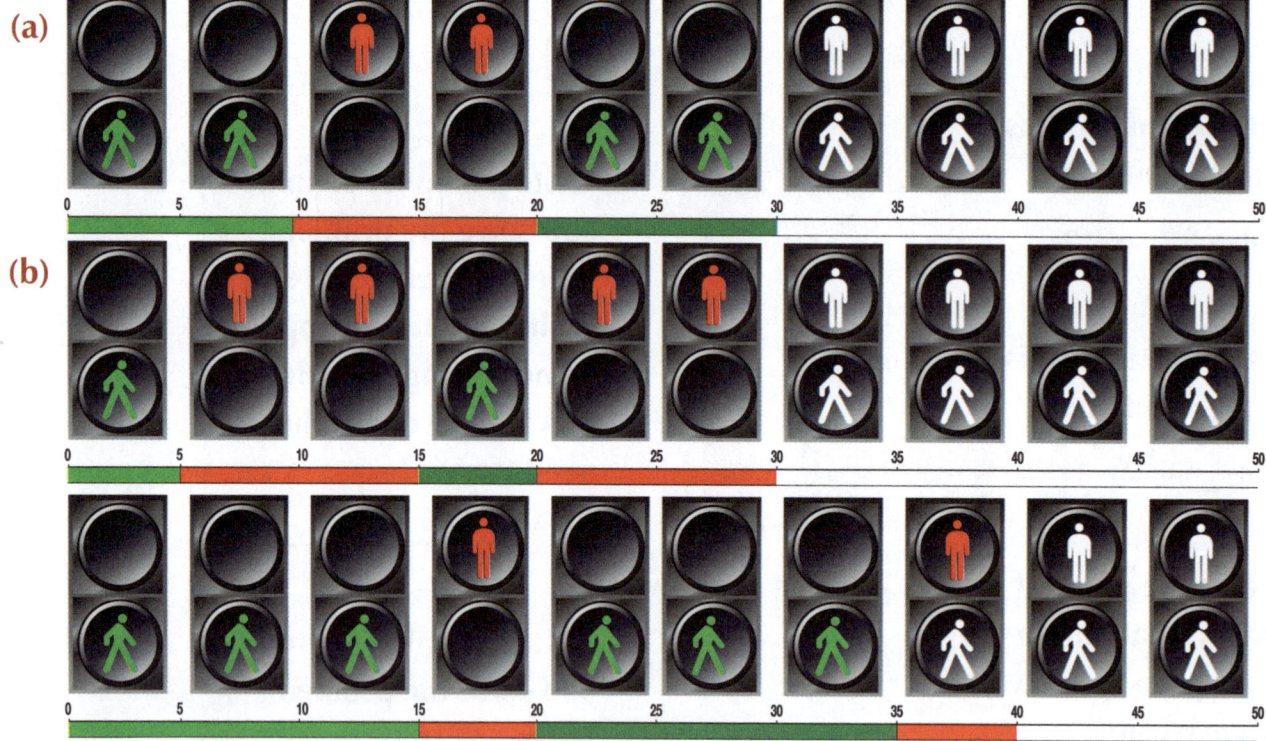

2. Now try these ones.

B. Try these

Read the newspaper article and answer the questions.

1. In what year was the first railroad in Ireland opened? How many years ago was that? _____
2. How many trains left Dublin every day for Dún Laoghaire? _____
3. Sleepers are used to hold the railway line.

   Sleeper

   (a) If sleepers were placed 1m apart on the tracks, how many sleepers are needed for 1km of track? _____

   (b) If sleepers were placed $\frac{1}{2}$m apart on the tracks, how many sleepers were needed for 1km of track? _____
4. How many pennies in a shilling? _____
5. How many 3rd class tickets could you buy for one shilling? _____
6. How many 2nd class tickets could you buy for two shillings? _____
7. On what date did the railway open? _____

C. In your opinion

1. Why should passengers not stick their heads out? Did all the carriages have windows? _____
2. What might the difference between 1st class and 2nd class be? _____
3. Is there still a rail link between Dublin and Dún Laoghaire? _____
4. Were trains more reliable or less reliable in 1834 than they are now? _____
5. Name something that is about 143cm long. _____
6. The journey took about 20 minutes. How long would it take to walk 10km? _____

Test yourself!

FUNPARK Admission Prices
- Adults €12·50
- Teenager €7·50
- Child €5·00
- Children under 4 free

1. How much will a family of 2 adults and 3 children (ages 2, 7 and 9) pay? _____

2. How much for 1 adult and 3 teenagers? _____

3. What change will I get from €50 if I pay for one adult, two teenagers and one 7 year old child? _____

4. A pair of jeans is usually €64. The jeans are reduced to half price in a sale. What is the sale price?
   - ☐ €30
   - ☐ €32
   - ☐ €128
   - ☐ none of these

5. A T-shirt is usually €30. The price of the T-shirt is reduced by one quarter. What is the sale price?
   - ☐ €7·50
   - ☐ €22·50
   - ☐ €7·00
   - ☐ none of these

6. The price of a jumper is usually €30. The price of the jumper is reduced to one quarter. What is the sale price?
   - ☐ €7·50
   - ☐ €22·50
   - ☐ €7·00
   - ☐ none of these

7. A gardener wishes to plant grass seed to make a lawn. He estimates that he will need at least $1\frac{1}{2}$ kg of seed. How many packets of seeds should he buy if a packet of seeds holds 400g? _____

8. At what time should Mum leave for a 4:30pm appointment if the journey will take 35 minutes and she wishes to call to her friend on the way for half an hour? _____

9. How many pages in 2 of these books? _____

10. How many pages in half of this book? _____

ROUGH WORK

ROUGH WORK